G000276024

FISHEYE
A guide to angling photography

First published in March 2012

All rights reserved. No part of this publication may be reproduced, stored
in a retrieval system, or transmitted, in any form by any means, electronic,
mechanical, photocopying, recording or otherwise, without prior
permission of the publisher.

© Text and pictures - Matt Hayes

© Cover design - Paul Moulder

© Design - Mpress (media) Ltd

Designed and published by m press (Media) LTD.

Unit Four, Ashton Gate, Harold Hill, Romford, RM3 8UF

Richard Lee

FOREWORD

ve spent over two decades in angling
urnalism attempting to prove that the 'pen
mightier than the lens' but I've finally
onceded that a good picture does indeed
aint a thousand words.

utside a handful of professionals in the
K, inspirational photography in the sport
f angling has largely been an underground
ovement with a membership you could
unt on one hand. Think fishing pictures
Britain, think man holds lump of meat.

s an all too bland a recipe that has
ecome more prevalent through the
opularisation of carp fishing. You've all
en the shot. Man cocks head at a 45
egree angle, stares longingly into the eyes
his capture, and shutter is depressed.
ever a more apt verb for the motion of
king one of those stale images.

cross the Atlantic in the States, the creation
imagery that celebrates the sport has
ankfully been more advanced as anglers
nted for the true essence of fishing, the
irit that unites those with an unrelenting
sire to cast carbon and cane. Those early
eatives realised the beauty of our banksides
further afield than a simplistic catch shot.

enics with huge skies that could transport
1 to the very moment the cast was being
de started to have an impact on the way
ne individuals chose to portray angling.

e man who has always shared the passion
depicting angling in all its splendour, and
o was at the forefront of the 'fishing
style revolution' in Britain, is Matt Hayes.

call in the early 90s, before the digital
olution had taken hold, standing
tionless at dusk on the banks of the
per Great Ouse as Hayes attempted to
ot the perfect moment. It was freezing
the East wind had started to punish

my bones, and my breath held in the air
like a thick smog.

Eventually, after ten painful minutes, Matt
declared 'he'd got the shot' and I could take
a break. Considering we'd landed three chub
over 6lb only hours earlier, I couldn't quite
comprehend how a silhouette of a man
grasping a rod and net was ever going to
surpass the hat-trick shot.

As it transpired, the instantly forgettable
catch picture did indeed make it into print,
but Matt's 'perfect moment' went on to
make several front pages and catalogues. It
inspired and connected with anglers, no
matter whether you were a game, salt or
coarse fisher.

Over the years Matt has developed the
ability not only shoot what it looks like, but
to shoot what it feels like.

Using all the advancements in cameras, from
SLRs to compacts to mobile phones, Hayes
has begun to explore the sport and started
to really see fishing in a deeper way.

It is a passion and a movement that is
starting to find a momentum in Britain and
Europe as more and more fishermen begin
to embrace photography and start to find
their own 'perfect moments'.

In this book, the first ever published in the
UK dedicated to 'angling photography',
Matt reveals the techniques he's used to
capture memorable moments in the UK and
Europe, whether that be a fish picture or a
breath-taking scenic.

Beauty by water can be seen by us all,
but seeing and composing that wild
beauty transforms the fun snap to a
photograph... Fisheye will help you make
that step forward.

Fisheye - A guide to angling photography

CONTENTS

The problem with writing a book like this is that things change and never more so than with technology. When I started to write, the idea of using Digital SLR cameras as movie cameras seemed very far off indeed: the fact that I had to add another chapter to the book because of the advances in HD movie features on DSLR's illustrates the problem.

A book like this would not have been a serious proposition several years ago. Angling photography has undergone a boom thanks to digital technology. In the far off days (it's not that long ago!) of film and transparency photography, few anglers bothered to carry a camera. Nowadays almost everyone has one, even if it is built into their cell phone. Nowadays it is possible to take a picture on the bank and have it on your 'Face book' page or uploaded to Twitter within minutes. You can even mail it to your friends, instantly!

Writing this book like has been like wrestling with a jelly: technology is changing so fast that being out-of-date within a very short period of time is constant danger. Each chapter has been reviewed prior to publication and brought up to date despite the fact that none of them had been written more than 12 months since. Thankfully, despite the digital era, whilst the cameras and the software bells and whistles might change, the basic skills of photography remain as relevant and important today as they always have been. The basic advice about framing, lighting, composition, apertures and shutter speeds will remain the building blocks of what separates simply taking snaps from photography. Key advances, however, are being made in low light performance of modern cameras and this is the area, in my opinion, where new possibilities to shoot handheld pictures that remain sharp and in-focus in situations that have proved impossible in the past.

This is a book for anglers everywhere. It tries to cover the subject of taking better photographs from an angler's perspective and, moreover, it gives advice from basic through to more advanced imaging. Whether you want to simply take better trophy shots with your camera phone, snap the odd decent landscape with your

serious outdoor photographer, this book is designed to help you bridge that gap.

I have tried to pour more than a decade of experience in serious photography into this book. In doing so, I am conscious that I am sharing knowledge that has given me an edge as a professional angler and photo-journalist. Whilst some of you will simply use the information to take better angling photographs, others will use the knowledge to help them in launching a professional or semi-professional career in sport fishing. Since I have always been driven to communicate how I feel about my passion, through film-making, words and images, I hope that by passing on some of this knowledge I am empowering others to do the same.

Without doubt, the hierarchical structures of the angling media are so much less relevant than they were even five years ago. Now the power to inspire and entertain is being driven not by design-heavy magazines or cost rich video companies but by passionate anglers armed with DSLR cameras. The cost of shooting, either stills or film, to a professional standard has dropped in real terms by hundreds of percent. Ever increasingly, the best images and films can be found on websites, Facebook pages, on the web, Vimeo or YouTube. There is a revolution going on and the modern era of digital photography has empowered all of us to be not just passionate anglers but photographers and film makers too. I am happy to have been a part of it...

RIGHT

This photograph illustrates the importance of composition and the positioning of points of interest within the frame. The shape and texture of the main boat is pleasing, providing a nice frame for the lure fisherman. The lure fisherman, in turn, provides a frame for the boat in the centre while in the background we have the rising sun. This is a classic example of how the eye can be led through the image by strong composition. There is so much to see and appreciate in this image that is not immediately obvious: the line of mist on the dam wall, the colourful clouds and the colours on the water. In my opinion, the wealth of points of interest and composition make this a classic

Chapter One

ANGLING AND PHOTOGRAPHY

One of the benefits of being an angler is that we get to see the natural world as few normal people ever get to see it. While the rest of the world sleeps or sits in commuter traffic we are by the water's edge, witnessing the mist-filled dawns and the fiery sunsets. We are awake and alert when the water birds break through the mist to poke among the weed beds; we witness the moment when the sun drops below the horizon and turns the water blood red; when the first bats take to silent wing and flit through the twilight like fleeting shadows we are by the waterside. While our nostrils are filled with the aroma of the water's edge: the water mint, the foam that breaks in the weir pool and the heady night scent of wild flowers, our ears detect sounds of water rushing over stone, of owls hooting in the nearby forest or pigeons cooing under the shade of the broad-leaved trees. Yet, the greatest thrill of being an angler is not that we are merely observers of nature, it is that we are part of it. We are wired into nature's plug socket in the most

unique way possible. And that is why an image of water is always more evocative if there is someone with a fishing rod somewhere in it.

Whilst many of us are happy just to be there when nature is at its finest there are those among us whom feel compelled to try to record what it feels like to be by the water and experience special moments so that others, both fellow anglers and non-fisherman, can feel how we feel. It is an impossible task, of course, but sometimes when we take a great photograph, some of that magic of what it was like to be there jumps out of the image and touches someone's soul...

Like many of you, I suspect that my interest in taking better angling pictures grew out of a desire to capture some of the magic moments that I have experienced while out fishing. At first, my ambitions extended only to taking better trophy shots but I soon came to realise that the true magic of angling lies in the places that

we fish in, the people that we fish with and the atmospheres that we experience. Capturing images that convey not just what has happened but what I felt are my priority. I want people to feel some of the emotion or the drama of the moment when they look at my photographs and I realise that trophy shots, whilst being nice to look at and great to brag about, generally lack impact. Taking angling photographs that contain so much of the joy and respect that I feel about angling required a major jump in photographic knowledge and technique. I went out, bought myself a better camera, a ton of slide film and went for it...

At first, of course, the results never quite matched up to the images I had in my head. I could see pictures OK but I didn't have the knowledge, skill or experience to translate them onto that tiny rectangle of 35mm film. I went through tons of film but occasionally I would get a shot right or discover something interesting by accident.

LEFT

This shot of Allan Sheppard with a fly-caught pike shows how a wide-angle lens can be used to produce a high impact image without making the fish or angler look 'grotesque.' Fill-flash has been used to retain the detail in the angler's face and reduce the shadows caused by the harsh contrast light. With the pike held forward it dominates the image and takes the eye through the frame. The angle is important - shot fully head-on with an ultra-wide angle lens the fish would look distorted and disproportionate. 14mm optically corrected lens, 1/160th sec at f8, ISO 50.

BELOW

Some shots lend themselves to a panoramic crop like this image of Jens Christiansen fishing the river Glomma in spring. Including an angler in landscape images makes them more interesting and landscape angling photography is very rewarding.

That is how it was to learn with film: the huge delay between when you sent the film away and got it back usually meant that you forgot what you were doing when you took the pictures and as a consequence learning was a slow and painstaking process. Nowadays, with digital cameras, learning is so easy - you can take a shot and review it instantly...

I wanted to capture those beautiful dawns when the sky is flooded with delicate pastel hues and the mist steams from the water; the blazing sunsets when the clouds tower above us and the heavens are on fire with colour; the spine-tingling moments when fish leap from the water and send water droplets scattering like diamonds on a glass tabletop. Since those early days, when I blundered along with my SLR camera and endless rolls of transparency film, I have learned enough to occasionally do justice to what I feel in my angling soul. It has been a painstaking road that has required some considerable effort: reading photo magazines and books; chatting to pro-photographers; experimenting endlessly and learning to handle post production techniques like Photoshop. How much quicker I could have got to where I am now if we'd had digital cameras back then! Moreover, I've spent a small fortune in camera equipment and invested endless hours waiting for just one shot.

Eventually, my passion for photography grew until it rivalled my love of fishing: it has never quite matched it but it comes close. Indeed, sometimes I am happy to spend time just taking pictures, not just fishing pictures. I love landscape, macro and nature photography. Yet I am never happier than when I am taking pictures that involve water, fish and fishermen.

Whether you simply want to take better catch or trophy shots; fancy capturing some scenic and action images; or maybe you crave to make the jump into capturing ultimate angling pictures, this book is for you.

Cameras and camera phones are now a standard part of every angler's equipment: not quite as important as a rod and reel, maybe, but one of the must-have pieces of kit even for pleasure fishers. With the advent of digital technology, taking angling photographs has never been easier - even your average mobile phone will take a pretty decent catch photograph.

RIGHT

As one salmon becomes fully airborne, a second fish leaves the water underneath it. The venue is the powerful Eggfossen waterfall on the Gaula river, Norway. This shot was achieved by hanging over the waterfall while fitted with a mountaineering harness. 28-70mm lens at 43 mm, 1/1000th sec at F4, ISO 400.

BELOW RIGHT

Big sunsets cry out for the silhouette treatment. Timing and light play a huge role in the impact of the image. At any other time of the day, this image would lack impact but the blood red evening sky and the inclusion of the structure in the image make it a classic.

LEFT

Dawn has just broken at Cragwood on Lake Windermere. A lone pike angler makes his first cast of the day from an anchored boat. Mist shrouds the water as the sun climbs above the tree line to flood the sky with brilliant, warm light. This shot is all about timing - five minutes earlier and the pastel colours in the sky would be shrouded by mist, five minutes later and the sun would have burnt away the mist. Who would not want to be part of a scene like this? 165mm, 1/750th sec at f5.6, ISO 200.

For most fishermen, recording a catch, so that it can be viewed by friends and family, is about the limit of their aspirations but there is a definite movement toward taking better angling pictures and I know that many of you reading this book want to go beyond the stereotypical 'man with fish' shot. Those of you whom own a decent compact camera will know that these pocket-size powerhouses are capable of punching way above their weight in terms of image quality and creativity. Modern digital SLR's (single reflex cameras) are, without doubt, a revelation.

I recently purchased a compact digital camera that's simply amazing. For Creative photography I still prefer by DSLR Canon's, but this mini powerhouse, the Panasonic Lumix FT3 is so good that I can recommend it to anglers everywhere. In addition to having a Zeiss lens of the highest quality it shoots 12 mega-pixel stills, is fully submersible and can be used underwater and also features an HD movie facility. For all but serious photography it's the ultimate piece of kit that can be zipped into a pocket and taken anywhere.

Digital is so good because it allows you to practice and review the results instantly. For anyone learning photography, gone are the days when you had to shoot a pile of transparency film, wait several days to get it back and then view a stack of images displaying various faults from wonky horizons to poor exposures. Nowadays you can delete poor images instantly. What's more, you can reframe until you are happy with the balance of the shot; try some fill-flash to gauge its effect on the image; avoid the messy tree branch that you failed to spot growing out of your fishing pal's head; re-focus so that the important parts of the image are sharp, not blurred and so on. What's also great about modern digital cameras is their ability to deliver good results when set to auto or 'idiot' mode. To take consistently good angling photos you will need to learn to switch auto off and use the camera on 'manual' but nonetheless, if you can learn how to see and frame and image properly, seven times out of ten your camera will deliver a pretty nifty result when set to auto.

So what makes a great angling photo? In my opinion, it's an image that goes beyond recording a catch or a scene: a great angling photo captures the magic, the atmosphere or the drama of angling. In other words, when someone else views it they feel something. More than anything else, when I see a great angling photo I want to be there and experience that moment for myself.

Catch photos of man-with-fish rarely cut the mustard - unless, of course, the fish happens to be of monumental proportions but then it's the size of the fish and the 'wow!' factor that makes it stand out. A catch photo can be considered successful if it happens to be pin-sharp with the fish well-displayed and with captor and quarry really well-lit. Sometimes a catch photo makes it to greatness if it's shot from an unusual angle or in an unusual way. A big fish, for example, can be made to look even more dramatic if it is held toward the camera (predatory fish often look really good displayed in this way) but it's a fine line between adding impact and going totally over-the-top with a wide-angle shot that makes captor and fish look slightly grotesque. Images of this type are used too frequently in the angling press these days and it's my opinion that they rarely have the impact that editors seem to think that they do. There is a danger with these 'in your face' wide angle shots that we are trying to change the emotion of angling and the nature of the fish that we are holding. Angling images that feel out of kilter with the moment or situation are always a flop. A benign or small fish displayed in such a way seems rather ridiculous to me.

RIGHT
The sense of isolation is profound when fishing on Argentina's Rio Grande, a Mecca for sea trout anglers. The landscape is barren and windswept. The driving force of the wind and the sound it makes as it howls across the plain is almost deafening, leaving the fisherman feeling alone in a desolate landscape. The black and white treatment given to this image attempts to capture that sense of isolation, and the use of a slight vignette around the edges of the image pulls attention toward the lone angler choosing a fly.

TOP LEFT

A low angle emphasises the gaping maw of a large catfish from the river Ebro in Spain. The red shirt adds a splash of colour and draws attention to a key area of the image. This is a classic example of how to make a trophy shot more interesting and impactful.

BELOW

I was fishing for trout in Arctic Sweden with my good friend Ed Brown when we got one of those sunsets that sends you scurrying for the camera. The breeze dropped to leave the lake becalmed and the distant clouds provided a wonderful anchor for the sunset. Ed hooked a fish as I was reaching for the camera leaving me little time for thought about treatment of the image. I settled for the classic silhouette to capture the rich colour detail and to freeze the action. The movement of the angler sends oily ripples in concentric circles - I often ask subjects to move slightly when wading in calm water to achieve this effect. This shot was taken using a panoramic camera, the Hasselblad X-Pan and shot on transparency film (Fuji Velvia). 45mm lens, 1/30th sec at f8, ISO 50.

Galleries of men with fish don't do it for me either. There is something rather anorak about row after row of grinning captors displaying fish with names and precisely recorded weights. Looking at them is rather like seeing someone else's holiday snaps or wedding photos - you lose interest after the third image. To an outsider they must look truly ridiculous and rather sad. Even worse are the captors that don't even smile and instead strike a pose that they feel makes them look mean and moody - a sort of fishing James Dean - when in reality they look rather silly.

The best angling catch shots are well lit, beautifully sharp, show the fish near to its environment and show the captor in a relaxed, happy or exuberant mood. A definite 'no-no' are the photos that I still see in magazines from some parts of Europe that show captors holding dead fish, usually suspended by its eye sockets. There is nothing even vaguely attractive or interesting about these photographs and all magazines should ban photographs of dead fish in my opinion.

Nonetheless, catch (aka 'trophy') photographs, whilst not at the most creative end of the angling photography, are a very important part of our sport. We all take them to remind ourselves of what we caught and, just as importantly to brag to our mates. In essence, they are part of angling history - national, international or simply sometimes just personal angling history. We owe it to ourselves to make the best job we can. And done in the right way, with the fish displayed in a creative way or being returned to its natural setting, catch photos can and do achieve greatness...

Usually, though, great angling images are those that convey mood, atmosphere or special moments. These are the images that capture the spirit of angling and make you want to go fishing when you see them. Whilst most of us are impressed by a picture of a big fish it rarely makes us want to go out there and do it. Show us an image of a lake at dawn shrouded in mist backlit by a fiery sun, however, and we all feel that longing to be a part of that scene rumbling in our gut...

As anglers we are in a privileged position when it comes to developing our photography skills. The truth is that photography is mainly about quality of light: light, the amount, type and direction can transform a mundane scene into a fantastic one in a matter of seconds. Dramatic light is usually seen at the extremes of the day - as anglers we spend a great deal of time out in nature at dawn and dusk. Even your local park lake can look absolutely stunning when the sun pokes its head above the horizon and sky and lake's surface are washed in a palette of stunning colours. Moreover, typical city dwellers just don't get to see the places that we regularly spend time in - being by water and surrounded by wildlife is part of the deal in angling and as such whenever we go fishing we are being constantly bombarded by a series of photographic opportunities.

Just how many of these opportunities that you grasp is your choice. Many of you, I suspect, simply want to take better catch photos or capture the glory of a favourite fishing venue. Others will want to go one or several stages further by capturing images that go beyond the basics. A few of you will already be competent photographers looking to turn that 'auto' or 'programme ' button on your camera off. To the latter group I say 'be warned!' Photography is seriously addictive. You will know that you've got it bad when you start picking the camera up when the light starts to fade and the fish usually start biting; your mates will get sick of you asking them to pose in landscape shots; you will curse every time a fish leaps out of the water and you don't have a camera in your hand.

Cameras have come a long way in recent years and so too has angling photography. Though the days of the guy holding the fish in a rag with a woodbine sticking out of the corner of his mouth, the top of his head cut off and his fishing gear strewn around in the background so that it looks as if he is standing on a bomb site are not quite yet gone, they almost are. There has never been a better time to take angling pictures and with the development of the DSLR as a film making tool, this really is the era when we ordinary folk have the equipment to compete with the professionals.

Chapter Two

THE KIT

One of the dangers of writing any book about photography is that it becomes too dry and technical. I will try to avoid making that mistake. If you are really serious about learning the technical aspects of photography there are numerous books out there written by far more technically competent people than me. Moreover, there are some great magazines that you can subscribe to that will teach you the mechanics of photography in an easily digestible and entertaining format. This is a book about angling photography and I will indulge in 'tech-speak' only when it is necessary to help you take better angling photographs.

Nonetheless, there is no escaping the fact that cameras, de facto, are complicated assemblies of modern technology. Even the digital camera on your cell phone is a sophisticated piece of equipment.

Fortunately, a lot of the technical 'wizardry' that goes into making modern cameras is designed to make them as simple to use as possible. It's my view that some of the worst cameras out there are the ones with a massive array of picture taking modes and functions and a guidebook that verges on war and peace.

Good cameras should be easy to use and after a while, intuitive. Indeed, I rarely use any camera on anything other than fully manual mode but to get to this stage requires a grasp of the fundamentals of photography (the subject of the next chapter). Cameras with lots of picture taking modes and fancy functions don't take better pictures than those that don't have them. What really counts, at the end of the day, is the camera's ability to take sharp, well-exposed photographs with plenty of detail.

Unavoidably I am going to have to use some 'photo-speak' when I talk about kit but I'll do my best to explain it in a way that I would have understood when I started out. I don't know about you but jargon has never been my strongest point.

There are three basic types of cameras used by anglers: camera phones, digital compacts and digital SLR's. The new breed of' ILC' cameras, (known as Interchangeable Lens Compacts), is going to be very popular with anglers too but so far the general public have not embraced them as much as the hype seemed to promise they would. Specialist cameras such as 35mm film cameras and medium format models will appeal to professionals, retro-camera fans and already-serious angling photographers. There is something special about a crisp, well-exposed transparency that, in certain light conditions, makes the image really zip.

RIGHT
Overnight frost has coated these trees that line the banks of the River Avon in Warwickshire. I took this shot from a boat jetty before launching for a morning's fishing. A polariser deepens the colour of the gorgeous blue sky. A polarising filter is one of the 'must have' filters for all photographers. 60mm, 1/90th sec at f8, ISO 100.

BELOW
This shot of Lake Windermere was taken just after dawn when the lake was flat calm. The colours are beautifully saturated and an ND grad filter has been used over the distant mountains and sky to balance the exposure with the foreground. Early and late are often the best times for images like this because the differences in luminance between sky, land and water are evened out by the soft, subdued light. 34mm, 1/4 sec at f16, ISO 50, ND Grad.

ABOVE
A late season pond olive captured on the Lumix FT3, this time using the macro function. A shot that just goes to show how good this compact camera really is.

Yet, with the advances in digital technology the gap has narrowed to be almost insignificant and in many cases digital images are now superior to the best that film can produce in almost any situation.

If you are determined, for example, to become a competent photographer, no matter what, a decent digital SLR with a good kit lens should be your choice. A digital SLR stands for Digital Single Lens Reflex camera. These are he cameras that you hang around your neck that sport a detachable lens and are used for serious photography. On the other hand, if you never want to go much further than some quality catch shots with nice 'scenic' and the odd 'grab' shot of something that catches your eye thrown in, digital compacts will serve you well. Some anglers, myself included, like to carry a compact for catch shots, especially when wading or covering large distances and a digital SLR when I've got the luxury of being able to keep all that kit with me. My Panasonic Lumix FT3 goes everywhere with me. For a compact camera it is quite remarkable, featuring Zeiss optic, 12 mega-pixel images, built-in flash submersible/waterproof functionality and HD movie function. Yet, despite being packed with all this technology, it still fits into a pocket. Amazing!

They say that fishing is all about a 'worm at one end' and a fool at the other. The same maxim holds true for photography; a perfect landscape might just as well be a rubbish dump if you can't see it. Even the best camera with the best lens won't take a great photograph unless you know how to use it. By the same token, a good photographer with an eye for a shot can take stunning images on a compact. Let's examine the three main types of imaging device or cameras.

LEFT
This image of my wife, Anne Marit, by the Fore
river in Norway illustrates how key subjects can be
framed either by structure, objects or, in this case
foliage. It is also a testament to how wonderful
modern digital cameras are. Just look at the range
of tones and colours that this image has captured.
24mm lens, 1/15th sec at f11, ISO 200

Camera Phones - Camera phones aren't really a serious proposition for anyone with more than a casual interest in photography. Despite the fact that the resolution on camera phones is getting better all the time, and they are getting easier to use, trying to fit a top quality lens into a credit-card slim device is currently impossible. Having said this, they have the advantage of being able to take a decent catch picture that can be downloaded onto a computer or attached to an MMS and sent to your mates almost instantly. And with the advances in technology coupled with the increasing sophistication of hand-held gadgets, cell phones that incorporate increasingly sophisticated compact cameras are being developed as I write.

To obtain half-decent results on a camera phone, you will need a built-in camera that offers a flash option and incorporates a decent number of mega-pixels to boost image quality. Three MP should be the minimum you should aim for but five or even six is better.

The serious disadvantages of camera phones are their difficulty of use, the fact that lens choice is limited, image quality is always compromised and the sensor simply isn't big enough to capture subtle detail.

Compacts - digital compacts are truly amazing. Pixel counts keep getting higher and higher, lenses get sharper and sensors are getting more sensitive. You can achieve some amazing results on compact cameras and they offer the advantages of improved image quality, better lens options with their built in zooms and they are much easier to use. Being light and compact, they are easy to fit into a pocket or fishing bag and you can even buy underwater housings for some compacts that extend their possibilities still further.

Indeed, there are now good compact cameras being advertised that are submersible down to the level of a few meters. A classic example at the time of writing is my beloved Panasonic FT3. These cameras are fantastic for anglers because it is a fact that keeping gear dry is a nightmare and there is the added bonus of being able to take underwater stills and movies.

Do not buy a camera just because it has an underwater capability – research its image quality both above and below the water. Also check out how wide the lens is – if it is not a wide angle you will have focusing and framing issues underwater and landscape imaging will be difficult.

RIGHT

I really like this image shot on an iPhone. The mist and stark outline of the tree give it an eerie, ethereal feel and the grain in the image does not look out of place on an image of this type.

BELOW

A pike photographed using a camera in a dedicated underwater housing. While some compact cameras can now be used underwater, the detail in this shot is strictly the preserve of a good DSLR. The underwater housing and twin strobe flashes used to light the fish are not cheap! 21mm, 1/80th sec, f6.3, ISO200.

ABOVE

Another camera phone shot, taken on the built-in camera on the iPhone. This one shows my dad fishing at sunrise when the first rays of light begin to burn off the mist. On a screen or used for the Internet, the image is fine. When blown up, however, the limitations of the camera phone become obvious.

It is a mistake to get too sucked in by the pixel-count war. Just because a compact offers more mega-pixels than its counterpart does not always make it a better camera. Mega pixels are a bit like engine cc's - in the old days the more cc's the engine had the faster the car went. That is, until the invention of fuel injectors, turbo chargers and engine management systems. Likewise, though pixel count is a decent indication of image quality, camera designers are now just as concerned with the type and size of the pixels and their ability to render colour and detail.

Many compact cameras now have a mega-pixel count greater than ten. Camera review sites and magazines will tell you just how well respective cameras perform. Suffice to say that you should look for a decent pixel count, a quality lens (some compacts now have Zeiss lenses!), quality built-in flash and variable ISO (film speed settings) along with shooting functions that allow you as much control as possible over aperture and shutter speeds.

As a general rule I would suggest that you beware of compact cameras that have too many functions. Most of these models excel at none of the functions they support. A camera with a pin-sharp wide angle lens with waterproof capability and a decent movie recording function would carry a hefty price tag.

At the time of writing, I own what I consider to be the ultimate compact on the market at the present time. It is water proof down to a depth of around sixty feet, shockproof, dust proof, takes images up to 13 megapixels in size and has a built-in lens of exceptional range and quality. To top it all, the camera has a video facility that records HD movies even when used underwater. Macro shots taken with the camera are impressive and yet it's wide angle lens is more than good enough for decent landscapes. It costs less than three hundred pounds and it is an amazing piece of kit. Made by Panasonic, it's small enough to fit into a jacket pocket or small corner of my tackle bag and I take it everywhere. And whilst it cannot compare with the superb quality of my DSLR it is close enough to be astonishing. It just goes to demonstrate how far digital cameras have come in a short space of time.

DIGITAL COMPACT
CHECKLIST

Pixel Count - 10 or more mp.

ISO - from 100 to at least 800.

Flash - both full and fill-flash options.

Red-eye reduction is useful for night-time catch shots.

Lens - most people look for a zoom but fail to pay attention to the wider end. I would always favour a wide angle lens over a telephoto zoom on a compact. 20mm is the benchmark at the wide end - the closer you can get to it the better.

Tripod Mount - very important for long exposure and low light shots.

Shooting modes - being able to switch to full manual is not an option traditionally offered by compacts but a good variety of shooting modes including landscape, portrait, low light, macro and sports is very useful.

Macro Feature - useful for capturing detail, insects and flies, baits etc.,

Files - most people shoot J-peg but some compacts are now offering a 'raw' file option. This is very useful for serious photographers whom use a digital compact periodically.

Underwater Capability – a great bonus but image quality is the number one.

Movie Function - really useful if you like to blog your fishing adventures.

LEFT
Compact cameras tend to work best in good light and fairly straightforward exposures. Low light or huge differences in exposure levels in the same scene tend to throw them out.

ABOVE

This landscape shot, taken with the Lumix compact, illustrates the capabilities of modern compact cameras. The picture is sharp, with excellent depth of field and has dealt with the contrast in the scene well. In terms of composition, the image illustrates the use of the river as a lead-in line to take the eye through the picture from the rocks in the foreground to the house in the background. The rocks and the house have been placed on the intersection points of an imaginary grid, consisting of three equally spaced horizontal lines and three equally spaced vertical lines. The intersection points of these lines are important areas to place key objects on because they create a composition that has balance and harmony.

RIGHT

A self-portrait with the Lumix compact sitting on a mini tripod, in this case a mini gorilla-pod. It has used fill-flash intelligently to compete with the strong backlit conditions. For a self-taken portrait, this is a nice result.

To complicate matters slightly, in recent years a new breed of camera, knows as 'Interchangeable Lens Compacts' have emerged. These are cameras that are a sort of half-way house between compacts and fully-blown SLR's, being light and compact yet offering interchangeable lenses. Not only are they now becoming more popular, they also fill a serious gap in the market for the person who wants small, neat camera with improved image quality and the ability to swap lenses.

Though these cameras are really mini SLR's and should be considered as such, they have serious possibilities for anglers because of their compact size and versatility. Whilst still considered a novelty by many serious photographers, they offer anglers the option to up go a stage beyond compacts without having to up the size of their kit bag or spend a fortune. As such, I take them very seriously and since technology is getting better all the time they are going to be serious contenders for your money if they catch the public's imagination and continue to be developed.

If these cameras have limitations, it's the fact that image quality is not ultimate, they are not as robust and pleasant to use as full size DSLR's and the lens options are not as good. When we consider 'ILC's' we can judge them by the standards of regular SLR's with the added proviso that some sacrifices in image quality and versatility are worthwhile to those whom want to carry as small amount of kit as possible or to use them as a 'bridge' camera to using a fully blown DSLR.

BELOW

This shot is remarkable because it demonstrate how great images can be obtained using compac cameras. This one was shot using the Panasoni Lumix FT3. Work in Photoshop/Lightroom i minimal but the detail has been drawn out using the tonal contrast tool. Flat, diffused light is ofter mistaken as poor for photography. For portrai photography, it is the best, allowing natura colours and textures to bloom.

DSLR's - digital single lens reflex cameras are simply a digital version of the single lens reflex (SLR) cameras used by photographers for many, many years. The early digital SLR's, though offering advantages over film SLR's always struggled to compete with a good transparency (slide) when it came to image quality. It is amazing, however, just how quickly DSLR's have closed that gap and, many would argue, have forged ahead. Some serious landscape photographers still use medium format film cameras because the big

transparencies they produce are beautifully colour-saturated and pin-sharp but I can't think of many that favour 35mm film over digital. The sheer detail of a 35mm digital file from a pro camera is now so staggering that it is hard for medium format film cameras to compete. Moreover, digital files are easy to edit, offering the photographer the option to tweak the image in terms of its exposure, colour saturation, sharpness and so on. Photographers no longer have to carry films of different speeds and types to obtain different looks and feels to their

images - they can simply dial in the ISO setting they want, shoot a picture and then convert it in Photoshop, Photomatrix, NIK Efex, Aperture or Lightroom to mimic the grain and saturation of any film going, including the best black and white. In short, not only have DSLR's caught up with the very best of film cameras, they offer a host of serious advantages that no other form of camera can compete with.

Like SLR's, DSLR's offer ultimate image quality and the ability to change lenses

changing the film and losing any unused frames). ISO is the film speed setting, calibrated for the original transparency and print films. Films were graded according to how quickly they would absorb light - the higher the ISO setting the faster the shutter speed that could be used in the same light. In regular conditions, film rated at ISO 100 was the regular choice of most photographers.

In Lower light or to obtain after shutter speeds, ISO 200 film enabled an extra f-stop of light. ISO 400 was twice as fast as ISO 200 and allowed two stops of light faster than 100. In very low light, ISO 800 and 1600 were used. Yet, with extra speed came a price: the faster the film, the 'grainer' the image. Yet, as I write, the latest Canon and Nikon cameras capture amazing images even In low light. Whereas grain was a problem with film cameras once one ventured beyond film rated at ISO 400, I have seen and taken digital images at ISO 800 or greater that exhibit negligible digital noise.

The latest DSLR's have got superb sensors that capture minute detail that even the best film SLR's would struggle to compete with. Couple these benefits with the fact that digital files are much more 'malleable' and Photoshop - friendly and you can appreciate why they are the camera of choice for serious photographers.

LEFT
A shot of the river Gaula in Norway. This is the home pool for our fishing lodge, the Winsnes Fly Fishing Lodge, and I have enjoyed photographing it in all of its moods through the seasons. Here a shift of the white balance to the cool end has given the image a slightly blue cast, emphasising the cold. It was minus sixteen! Shots like this require the use of a tripod to obtain a sharp exposure with a good depth of field. 16mm, f11, 1-second exposure.

BELOW
Modern tube flies tied by Matt Hayes displayed next to an old bottle left behind at the Winsnes Fishing Lodge in Norway by the British gentry, aka 'Salmon Lords.' Using a homemade 'studio' consisting of net curtains to act as diffusers, a glass tabletop and coloured card underneath the glass, I was able to create this memorable shot using a fill light and off-camera flash. Sometimes it is not always necessary to spend a fortune on kit to get professional-looking shots! 100mm, 5 seconds at f16, ISO 50.

There are medium format digital backs that will produce even higher quality images but they are pretty impractical for field use other than when mounted on a tripod for a landscape or wild life shoots that have been set-up in advance. They are also incredibly expensive. A good digital back will cost in excess of 10000 pounds and as much as twenty thousand plus.

With a DSLR you get the added advantage of being able to alter ISO settings with every shot you take if you wish (with a film SLR this means

This shot shows the glorious detail that a compact camera cannot hope to cope with. This is a classic DSLR shot using a wide-angle F2.8 lens, slight under-exposure of the image and the use of fill-flash to expose the subject. The amount of detail in the file is remarkable, and some careful tweaking of the raw file has resulted in a final image in which lots of fine detail has been drawn out.

DSLR s still use ISO setting but instead of film grain, higher ISO settings produce digital noise'. However, the performance of DSLR's in low light conditions is now so good that it has become one of their defining triumphs over film-based SLR's.

The latest benefit to using digital SLR's is the option to shoot HD quality movies with them. This is an important benefit to a growing army of fans. The results obtained with the latest digital SLR's are nothing short of staggering. Though less intuitive and easy-to-use than camcorders or movie cameras, the ability to use a choice of lenses delivers a feel to the quality of the footage shot on Digital SLR's that no other medium can match.

This is especially true for shallow depth-of-field or ultra-wide stuff. Pioneers like Philip Bloom have turned movie making with DSLR's into an art form and demonstrated the huge potential of the medium. Predictably, the camera manufacturers have begun to exploit the movie making capabilities of a CMOS sensor of the type used in the Canon 7 D and the 5D MK 2 to produce movie cameras that will redefine movie making.

Whilst these emerging cameras such as Canon's pioneering C300 are considerably more expensive than a regular DSLR, they are astonishingly cheap when compared to end movie cameras of old. The quality of image they deliver is way ahead of even the best camcorders and the issues that surrounded the first movie making DSLR's have been thoroughly addressed.

So what should you look for in a good DSLR? As I mentioned earlier, whilst it might be good for a novice to have a camera that works very well in auto or 'programme' mode, I consider an array of fancy shooting modes as being of little, if any benefit. Once you have learned how to meter and understand light, you will shoot on manual most of the time anyway. There are a few useful programme modes, however and one essential one: bulb. Bulb is the setting that allows you to leave the shutter open for as long as you like by manually opening and closing it - vital for night photography.

Modes - P or Auto, bulb, AV. TV is borderline useful for stills but vital for movie making.

Flash - built-in flash is quite useful for fill-flash but top-end DSLR's need a dedicated flashgun.

ISO - range from 100 to 800 is essential. Low (ISO 50) is desirable. Some cameras boast ISO ranges up to more than 100,000 but 1000 seems to me to be the limit for quality results. (This situation will improve massively in the years to come).

Lens - if the camera comes with a kit lens, make sure that the lens is a decent one. The most useful lens for anglers is somewhere around 18-55 or 24-70. Bear in mind that unless you buy a full-frame sensor DSLR the focal length of the lens will be multiplied by 50%, making the 18-55 a 27 - 82.5mm. There is some really good kit lens deals available so if you shop around so don't buy the first camera kit you see.

Image Quality - the higher the 'pixel count' the better, generally, but don't get sucked into the view that MP count is everything. Read the camera reviews in photo magazines and on the internet if you want to find out how good image quality really is. The quality of the sensor and the type of pixels are just as important as the pixel count.

Build Quality - the reviews often major in on this area and it is well worth the attention. As anglers we spend a lot of time in the damp and semi-hostile conditions so the build quality of the camera is important.

Handling - how easy is the camera to use? Are the dials and functions tricky to use or intuitive? How easy will they be in the dark?

Screen - the bigger the playback screen and the better the resolution it offers the better. Live view shooting is useful for novices and when you lend the camera to friends for a trophy shot of you. Live view is also essential for movie-making.

Cleaning - sensors that offer self-cleaning are very useful. Sensors attract dust every time you change lenses and cleaning them manually takes knowledge and care. Self-cleaning sensors vibrate every time you turn the camera on and off, shaking the dust away.

Shooting Modes - make sure that the DSRL you buy offers both J-PEG AND RAW shooting modes. All new cameras will do this but some older second hand models may not offer RAW. Special black and white file capturing options are pointless because creating mono images from colour is easy in Photoshop.

Drive - how many frames per second will the camera handle? Five, seven or up to ten frames per second is the benchmark of a good digital SLR. Having a good FPS count is critical if you want to photograph fast moving subjects such as casting or fish jumping.

Buffer Speed - this is the speed with which your camera takes the pictures, processes the files and prepares for the next shot or shots. This is the most frustrating thing about older cameras, be they compact or DSLR - it is poor buffer speed that creates that awful delay between pressing the shutter and the camera taking the picture.

Sometimes this delay can be painfully long, causing you to miss a vital shot. Check that the camera's buffer speed and general performance are fast.

Movie Capability – some of the top end DSLR's now have movie capabilities that are staggering. Check the quality of the file the camera can produce: HD quality at 16.9 is the benchmark. If making movies with a DSLR is important, also consider how easy the camera is to use in movie mode. How easy is focusing, for example?

AV (Aperture priority) and TV (shutter priority). With AV you dial in the aperture and the camera calculates the shutter speed to match it and in TV you dial in the shutter speed you want and the camera calculates the optimum aperture that shutter speed will handle. TV is especially useful if you intend to use the camera to shoot movies. Other than these modes I can't think of any that you will really need if you understand the basics of photography.

Before leaving the subject of camera choices to look at accessories, I must mention another serious contender for the angler's money, the Go Pro Hero series of mini cams. These amazing little devices come with a choice of housings to protect the camera and allow sound or a completely sealed unit that allows the camera to be submerged in water. Featuring a fixed wide-angle lens, they capture decent stills and even record HD movie footage!

They can be taken just about anywhere and feature a variety of mounts that enable the user to strap them to their head, chest, surf board, bike, boat, pole or tripod. These cameras have a big future in angling because they are superb devices for making video blogs and capturing stills even in tricky situations. The latest versions can be linked to shoot full 360 degree images. Amazing!

Having kitted yourself out with a good camera, the next stage is to consider the accessories you might need. The most important are a decent cable release if you own an SLR and some means of supporting the camera for self-photography or long exposure shots. Most people favour a tripod but there are specialised mini pods such as the 'Joby Gorrilapod' that are very good with small

cameras. I have recently discovered a highly versatile mini-pod known as the 'Trek-Tech' by Optera. A tripod is essential not just for a DSLR but also for a good compact. The smaller and lighter the camera the smaller and lighter the tripod capable of supporting it.

These two important pieces of kit are essential if you want to do any self-portrait catch photography, landscapes or low light/night shots. This is because in certain situations hand holding the camera will result in camera shake. Even a small amount of movement when you depress the shutter will create a blurred image

unless you are using fast shutter speeds. For example, you might want to shoot a fishing scene where everything in the image, from front to back is sharp. The amount of sharpness throughout the image is known as depth of field. If you want everything, from the closest to the furthest away objects in the image to be sharp you will need to use a narrow aperture (such as f16) to achieve the desired result. Narrow apertures have to be coupled with longer exposures and it is rare that you will encounter conditions whereby you can shoot hand held at F16 without compromising the image quality. Sometimes, even with narrow depth of field, whereby you want the subject to be sharp and the background reduced to a blur (shallow depth of field), you will need a tripod if the light values are low.

Many night shots require the use of a tripod because of the long exposures involved. As a general rule of thumb, when the shutter speed in hundredths of a second is longer than the focal length of your lens (expressed in mm) the camera should be secured to a tripod. For example, a 100mm lens with a shutter speed of 1/60th of a second should be tripod mounted while at 250th second hand-holding is fine.

ABOVE

This high altitude Norwegian lake is a favourite of mine for char fishing. On this occasion, after stowing my gear at sunset, I set up the tripod to photograph this awesome twilight scene. The sun had dipped below the mountains an hour before, but the afterglow is very strong. The undersides of the clouds are still lit warm pink and peach while the rest of the sky is filling with stars. Over the distant mountains, the aurora begins to dance… 25 seconds at f4, 14mm lens, ISO 400.

LEFT

A wonderful image that illustrates just how much detail a modern DSLR camera can capture, even in the dark. With each passing year, the low light performance of modern digital cameras is advancing at an amazing rate. Canon's new release, the 1DX, makes it possible to take hand-held shots in almost pitch darkness. This shot, taken on one of its predecessors, nonetheless demonstrates just how good the modern digital sensors used on these cameras are.

un experienced photographer will be able to hand hold the camera at lower shutter speeds than a novice but the difference might be just one or two stops. Resting the camera on a fence, rock or other form of support will help with hand-held shots but everyone has a limit and the longer and heavier the lens the more pronounced camera shake problems become.

When mounted on a tripod, the shutter should be released either on the camera's built-in timer or, better still, a cable release (remote cord). This reduces the chance of the camera moving while the shutter is open.

Tripods are very important. I own several, reserving the use of the larger, more sophisticated models for days when I don't have to travel great distances with the camera and a more compact, lightweight model when roving and fishing. A good tripod will be light, sturdy and stable. Carbon fibre models are the best but they are expensive and lightweight aluminium is a decent substitute. A good fishing tripod will have independently adjustable legs to cope with sloping banks and a tilt and pan head to enable you to point the camera in almost any direction without having to shift the tripod. The very best tripods feature a removable centre column, enabling the user to position the camera very low to the ground for creative and macro shots.

Memory cards are an often-overlooked feature of DSLR cameras. I would recommend a memory card with a capacity of at least 2GB for angling photography because if you are out for more than a few hours you might need to store a lot of shots before you can download them. Cards up to 64gb are now available. If you intend to shoot movies in HD, professional flash and SD cards are. Must due to their superior writing speed.

Filters are often talked about by budding photographers and all of us, I think, go through a 'filter phase' where we try fancy filters such as starbursts, fog, tobacco etc; until we become bored with the novelty factor. In serious photography, there are filter techniques

frowned upon. Generally speaking, if you can see at a glance that the shot has been heavily filtered the photographer has failed. There are lots of photographic filters - some essential, some useful and some so specialised that they might be considered next to useless. Most digital imaging software packages such as Photoshop now come with digital filters that whilst perhaps not quite as effective as filters used when the photo was taken, will get you out of jail. These are especially useful with compacts because compacts cannot currently be fitted with lens mounted filters.

FILTERS AND THEIR
USES IN ANGLING
PHOTOGRAPHY

Skylight: a very popular choice. Technically it filters out UV light but most people use them to protect the lens.

Warm-up: a useful filter to make images warmer (applies a warm cast to the whole image).

Polariser: a circular (not linear) polariser is probably the most important filter of all. It darkens and deepens blue skies, removes haze/reflections and saturates colours. Note that the use of a polariser will cut back the light passing through the lens by two stops, leading to longer exposures.

ND (Neutral Density Filter): this is a neutral grey filter available in different strengths (0.3, 0.6. 0.9 and 1.2 stops). It holds back light without affecting image quality or colours. This filter is really useful if you want to photograph moving water or waterfalls and reduce it to a dreamy blur.

Graduated ND (Graduated Neutral Density): this filter works like a standard 'ND filter.' It is suitable for a wider variety of effects, however. The neutral grey coating is applied to just half of the filter and also with a coating that increases in density the further up the filter it goes. At the top, the grey will be quite dark, fading to very opaque near the centre of the filter. Its use is to hold

back light in portions of the scene, usually the sky, when one half of the image is much brighter than the other.

With a bright sky, for example, the light is held back by the grad filter, allowing for a more evenly balanced exposure and a more natural looking photograph. Because the coating is applied in a graduated manner, softening in opacity, its use will not be obvious in the finished image. This is a must-have filter for landscape photographers and carrying variety from 0.3 stops to 1.2 is commonplace.

Chocolate Grad: this is a lovely filter for warming up autumn colours and giving them real punch. Not used too often but a killer in the right circumstances.
Tobacco Grad: often used to create men-looking stormy skies but one of the most obvious and abused filters of the lot. Use it sparingly or not at all.

Coral Stripe: a nice filter for adding a stripe of colour to a slightly insipid sunset.

Twilight: in certain conditions, daylight can be made to look like twilight with the careful use of these special filters but they are limited in use.

Starburst: a gimmick filter easily mimicked in Photoshop. Don't bother. Mist: as above. There are some decent Photoshop Plug-Ins that mimic mist but I've found that if the mist isn't there don't put it in because it won't look right.

Filters - here a red filter has been used to add extra colour to this sunset silhouette. Their use must be controlled, however. Over-saturation can produce rather garish images. In my view, this image is on the borderline.

If you are interested in filters, both Cokin and Lee make excellent ranges. Circular lens mounted filters simply screw onto the lens (make sure that you get the right size for your lens) while the resin grad and ND filters need to be mounted in a filter holder. This consists of a ring that fits onto the lens and a holder that accepts one or more filters. Check out the Lee website for more information.

Always keep your kit in a bag to protect it from damp, dust and grit. Fishing trips can be harsh on cameras and you owe it to yourself to protect your camera and lenses. Hard-core angling users will appreciate the ultimate in waterproof protection offered by some of the Lowepro rucksacks that feature a waterproof zip and seal system.

Finally, a camera cleaning kit, comprising a blower brush, soft lens cloths, lens fluid cleaner, baby cotton buds and lens filter tissues is essential. Cleaning your camera and lenses regularly really will pay dividends, especially with modern cameras that have so many electronic components. Damp is an enemy to your camera so remember to take it out of your fishing bag between trips and store it in a warm, dry place.

DSLR sensors nowadays feature self-cleaning mechanisms but if you change lenses regularly you will encounter the irritating phenomenon of sensor dust. These are small particles and hairs that find their way onto the sensor and show up in images. While self-cleaning sensors help, cleaning the sensor from time to

time is essential. There are now some excellent kits and sensor cleaning swabs available.

If you are going into the movie business with your DSLR there are some accessories that are useful. A tripod is essential. Invest in a 'pod' that allows you to pan fluidly without shake or hesitation. For timelapse photography, a device known as a slider is a very useful piece of kit that will make your time lapse movies look really professional. Other accessories that are useful if you want to produce commercial quality footage are aids to focusing smoothly (focusing rings), camera shoulder mounts and panning accessories. Details of these can be found on Philip Bloom's website: www.philipbloom.co.uk or on the Zacuto website.

Whilst the camera body can be seen as the photographer's memory (its job being to record data about the image), lenses are the photographer's eye. They help us interpret and capture images from scenes, filtering out unwanted detail and accentuating those parts of the scene that we want to include. With wide angle lenses we can create space; with long lenses we can isolate key details; with regular medium lenses we can create flattering portraits. Every scene or object can be interpreted in a different way by shooting with a different lens, making lenses very important indeed...

Moreover, lenses are the most vital and probably expensive accessory that you can buy for your camera. They are almost as important if not more important than the camera body that you attach them to.

That is why they have a chapter of their own. There is no point in owning an expensive camera with a good sensor if the lens you couple it with delivers soft or dull results. A good lens will deliver sharp, crisp images throughout its focal range. This is an especially important consideration with zoom lenses that allow you to go through a variety of focal lengths.

The final quality of the image delivered by the lens is dictated by the build quality and the number and quality of the optical elements. Some lenses feature built in motors to help them focus and these should be silent and fast, locking focus as fast as you can point and shoot. The very best long lenses (telephotos) feature image stabilising technology (small motors that are built into the lens to reduce the effects of camera shake).

Needless to say good lenses are expensive, in some cases more expensive than the camera body. This is because a lens is a precision piece of optical equipment - every lens element has to be flawless and perfectly ground/polished.

Top quality lenses can operate in very low light by having a wide aperture range, usually from f2.8 or f4 up to f22. They allow more light into the viewfinder, producing a brighter image in all light conditions. All DSLR lenses will display their focal range and f-stop range. Typically the lens will be classed in focal length (mm) and f-stops. An example is a 28-70mm f4-5.6. This means that the lens is a zoom model that operates at 28mm at its widest and 70mm at its longest length. It operates at a range of maximum f-stops varying from f4 to f5.6. Remember that most DSLR's do not have a full-frame

sensor and you must add 50% to the focal lengths of the lens to get its genuine operating length. A 28-70mm lens truly operates at 42 - 105mm on most DSLR's.

It is possible to have two lenses that operate at 28-70mm with one lens being significantly superior to its rival. A lens with a maximum aperture of f2.8 will permit more light to enter than the same lens rated at f4-5.6. This jargon means that if you use the latter lens at its wider range (28mm) it can be used at f4 while at the top end (80mm) the widest aperture you can use it at a widest aperture of f5.6. On the other hand, an f2.8 lens will operate at maximum aperture (f2.8) throughout its focal range. These so-called 'fast' lenses not only operate in lower light at faster shutter speeds, the size of the front element will be much larger, pulling in more light in

all conditions and delivering sharper images in all light conditions.

Not all zoom lenses will deliver good edge sharpness at all focal lengths and throughout the focal range. Most will deliver good sharpness and detail in the centre of the image in all conditions but when you push the lens to the extremes of the f-stop ranges and focal lengths the edge sharpness and detail will suffer in all but the best. I have noticed a huge improvement in edge sharpness and a reduction in distortion with the latest ranges of Canon lenses, for example.

Most serious photographers get locked into the lenses they use by the camera manufacturer. As a Canon user I use Canon Lenses and the more lenses I own the less likely I am to buy a Nikon camera body because the lens mounts

for the two brands are different. Third party manufacturers like Tamron and Sigma make lenses with a choice of mounts to fit Canon or Nikon but there is no such thing as a dual mount. Once Nikon or Canon have got you locked in the chances are that your lens kit will keep you locked in for a very long time. Not that this is a bad thing because both Canon and Nikon make fantastic lenses and cameras.

This 'loyalty' to certain manufacturers is likely to increase with the development of the latest movie cameras that use DSLR sensors. Camera bodies such as the C300 by Canon can be used to record sumptuous HD movie footage with top-end Canon lenses. There are, however, conversion rings that allow the mounting of Nikon lenses on Canon bodies and vice-versa.

LEFT
One of angling's magic moments captured on a long lens. A bonefish tail against a mangrove backdrop while chasing the last shrimps exposed by a falling tide. Without a long telephoto lens, in this case, a 300mm lens, images like this are impossible. Shots like this sum up the magic moments that anglers cherish.

ABOVE
On this occasion, I used a polarising filter to cut back some of the glare on a bright sunny day and to deepen the colour in the sky. Fill-flash, with the flashgun mounted off the camera took care of the harsh shadows that are a hallmark of this type of light. Using a medium-length prime lens, in this case 35mm, I avoided any distortion effects that one often gets with wide-angle lenses to create a very natural-looking portrait. 35mm, 1/125th sec, f6.7 ISO 100.

Prime or Zoom?

The first thing that you will have to decide when you choose lenses for your camera is 'prime' or zoom? Prime lenses have a fixed focal length, for example, 50 or 100mm. A zoom operates at different focal lengths, say, from 16-35mm. At first glance it's a no-brainer, surely? After all, the zoom lens is more versatile, covering a range of photo lengths. Yet zooms are not without their downsides.

Typically, a zoom will not deliver razor sharp results, edge-to-edge, throughout their entire focal range. They are also invariably more expensive. Moreover, although the gap is closing, prime lenses are traditionally held to be sharper than their zoom counterparts. An f2.8 50mm is much cheaper than an 18-55mm 3.5-5.6 and it will probably be sharper too. As an angler you might also like to consider what happens when you give one of your mates a DSLR with a zoom lens and ask him to take a trophy shot for you. Trying to explain how to work the zoom and the autofocus can be an exercise in frustration - give them more than one thing to think about and the trouble starts...

RIGHT

The best angling images convey a mood or feeling about a moment or place. On this occasion, I was fishing with my wife, Anne Marit, on a very remote section of a mountain river. The sense of peace and solitude was overwhelming and that's why I opted to feature Anne Marit as a tiny figure casting against a huge landscape. This type of shot is a classic for a wide-angle lens because they open up the image and convey a huge sense of space. The shot is only possible because the sky is interesting - the same image on a day when the sky lacks colour or texture would simply look dull, uninviting, and uninspiring. Sensing the right mood for the image and tailoring the photograph to match the light conditions on the day is vitally important. On days when the light is flat and dull or the clouds are washed out, I try to crop out the sky. 24mm lens fitted with a polarising filter, 1/30th sec at f11, ISO100.

ABOVE

Professional pike angler Mick Brown with a huge reservoir pike. This is a beautiful trophy shot in which photographer and subject have worked together. The fish is displayed superbly while at the same time held safely. Mick is in the water and if the pike struggles it will not fall on a hard bank. The framing is very tight - angler and fish fill the image. The exposure is spot-on and the use of fill-flash has added some extra sparkle and punch. This is probably my favourite catch or trophy shot and it is no coincidence that it was taken with a classic portrait lens, a 50mm 1.4. Prime 50mm lenses can be obtained at bargain prices and yet they deliver pin-sharp, flawless images. For catch photography they are probably the best lenses of all and all anglers should carry them. 50mm, 160th second, f5.6, ISO 100. Fill-flash set manually.

LEFT

A macro lens is very useful for capturing key detail and in this case for still-life portraiture. A prime 50mm or 100mm lens renders beautifully sharp images. Prime lenses still probably have a slight edge over zooms in terms of image quality but the gap is closing.

This image of an angler fishing in the evening on the magnificent Stryn river on Norway's west coast sums up why we go salmon fishing, The mountains dominate the image as the last rays of the setting sun paint the peaks with warm colour. Here a long 200mm lens has been used to shoot the image from a nearby bridge. Notice how the lens has compressed the distance between the angler and the mountains in the background, making the landscape appear to loom over the subject. A wide-angle lens would have not achieved this effect. 70-200mm lens at 105 mm, 1/30th sec at f5.6, ISO 200.

all they have to do is step nearer or further away until they get the frame right and the whole job is easier. The prime is invariably shorter and lighter than the zoom and the resulting reduction in camera shake is an added bonus. For these good reasons, I often fit a prime to my camera when asking an inexperienced photographer to get a grab shot for me. As a photographer, prime lenses will make you think harder about camera positioning and angles. Prime lenses focus your mind on seeing scenes with certain focal lengths – no bad thing.

Movie makers will also find fixed focal length prime lenses appealing. They deliver superb, pin-sharp results and are especially favoured by purist film fanatics.

Having waxed lyrical about prime lenses, I must confess to owning a number of zoom lenses for my stills work. Some of the top Nikon and Canon zooms are getting better all the time. The 70-200mm Canon f2.8, for example, is an incredible lens that delivers pin-sharp results throughout its focal range. Ditto the 28-70mm and the 16-35mm.

For most users, I think, zooms deliver superb results and they are much more versatile so unless you are going to get really serious and are prepared to carry a large number of lenses, stick to the zooms. For most anglers zoom lenses are more versatile and mean carrying less kit but I would suggest carrying at least a 50mm prime for catch photos (other people will find it easier if they don't have to worry about zooming and the results from a lens of this type are unbeatable with trophy shots).

Rather than run through every lens available to man, I will list the lenses I use for my photography and try to evaluate their usefulness. Bearing in mind that I am a serious photographer, almost all of the lenses I own are f2.8 or faster - lenses of this quality simply are not necessary for casual use. You should also bear in mind that my camera bodies are full-frame sensor models so they do not alter the focal length of the lens. Most DSLR's increase the focal length of the lens by 50% and you should bear this in mind when making comparisons. What I mean by this is that with most digital cameras, a 16-35 mm lens will actually operate at 24 – 42.5mm.

LEFT

Great use of a wide-angle lens. The slight curvature is the result of barrel distortion that is common with wide lenses. Here it does not distract from the image. The shot is beautifully framed and the viewpoint has been carefully chosen to prevent the fish from looking out of proportion. Wide-angle lenses are important when taking trophy shots in boats, and the captor has a vital role to play in the quality of the final image: the fish needs to be held close to the body to prevent the fish looking grotesque.

ABOVE

Magic in miniature! A small fish can be just as remarkable as a specimen if it is given the right treatment. Here the beautiful colours of the juvenile perch have been captured and the red holographic bloodworm fly adds an extra splash of colour without proving distracting. 100mm lens, 1/400th sec at f6.3, ISO 100, fill-flash.

RIGHT

Wide-angle lenses are terrific for capturing shots that have a sense of space, placing the angler within the 'bog landscape.' Here a polarising filter has been used to deepen the blue in the sky.

Wide Angle

Wide angle lenses really are vital for creative angling photography. Action, dramatic catch shots and fishing landscapes all lean heavily on wide angles.

10-22mm: this is an ultra wide angle lens designed for non full-frame sensor (most DSLR's other than 'Pro or Semi-Pro' models. I bought one for one of my back-up cameras that does not have a full-frame sensor. On a regular DSLR this lens has an effective focal range of 15 - 33mm. This is a great choice for ultra wide angle work.

14mm: this is a prime lens I use with my pro DSLR'S. While most lenses that are this wide are fisheye lenses, this one is optically corrected and so is better. I get really dramatic shots with this lens but you have to know how to control the distortion of an ultra wide-angle lens like this one.

15mm fisheye: a speciality lens that curves the image around the edges, creating a very funky-looking wide angle effect. This is a model that needs to be used sparingly.

16-35mm: this is my 'go-to' wide-angle zoom. On a full frame DSLR, 16mm is plenty wide enough and 35mm is erring toward a decent portrait length. A very useful lens for landscapes, action and portrait shots when you need to get close and still pull in plenty of background.

24mm prime: a nice, short, thumb nose moderate wide-angle lens that delivers very sharp results. It is especially good for landscapes when a polariser is fitted and because it is so short and light it is easy to get sharp hand-held shots in quite low light.

24mm Tilt and Shift: this is a speciality lens that is mainly used for architecture and indoor building photography. The tilt and shift functions correct distortions in perspective created by regular lenses (often these are called 'converging verticals'). The result is straight edges that are not straight (pillars, edges of windows and buildings or rooms) that narrow. Whilst not a classic lens for angling photography, I use mine for certain shots where a low or high camera angle is useful.

Medium Lenses

50mm prime: a great portrait lens. Really nice results can be obtained when using this lens for trophy shots. It's short and light making it great for hand-holding. Results are razor sharp. The added bonus is that an f1.8 50mm can be picked up for a lot less than most zooms. This is the perfect lens to fit when novices grab your camera for a catch shot.

28-70mm: I use this lens a lot, especially on my full-frame sensor pro-cameras. If I used regular DSLR's more regularly I would probably favour the 18-55mm range because of the increase in focal length. Lenses like these are worth their weight in gold: good for catch shots, nice for landscapes and with a long enough top-end length to crash in for some detail when needed.

18-55mm: this has become a very popular kit lens for cameras without a full-frame sensor. On such models, it carries an effective focal length of 24 - 83mm, making it the non-pro camera version of the 28-70mm.

ABOVE

This shot of top angler Terry Hearn was taken with a 50mm lens. These are probably the most useful lenses for any angler to own for taking catch or trophy shots and they are cheap! The image is clean, lacking any distortion, well exposed, sharp, and crisp. Fill-flash has blown away some of the shadows caused by the harsh winter light. 50mm, 1/125th sec, f4, ISO 160.

LEFT

A damselfly has landed on the oar of the boat. The macro lens used to take this shot is capable of producing stunning images with amazing details and colours. 100mm macro lens, 1/200th sec at f11, ISO 200.

Long Lenses

100mm macro - verging on the longer length, I debated which category suited this lens best. Anyhow, it's a great lens for close-up macro work and it also takes great portraits. I use it on a full frame DSLR but a regular body would take it up to 150mm increasing its performance as a long zoom. I get some great shots with this lens and if you are the sort of angler whom spends a lot of time sitting in the same place for hours or days on end you will have bags of fun photographing insects, rig bits and plants with a macro.

65mm Macro – this is a speciality Macro lens recently introduced by Canon. It is far from easy to use and manual focus only but the results are amazing! It is possible to take images that are five times

life size and from distances of just a few millimetres. For ultimate detail work when photographing insects, this is a fantastic toy!

70-200mm: a fantastic lens that delivers sharp results no matter what focal length I use it at. On a standard DSLR this would become a 105-300mm. The shallow depth of field makes it perfect for picking out subject against the background.

100-400mm: I get decent results with this lens but it's not as sharp as the 70-200mm. I think that this is typical of all lenses that try to cover too great a focal range. I tend to restrict its use to hiking sessions when I feel I should carry a long lens but saving weight and space are priorities.

BELOW

Here a 200mm lens has been used to pick Mick Brown out of the background. With so much foliage behind him, a wide angle or conventional lens with the camera set to auto would have created an image where the confusing background competed with the main image. Long lenses, from 100mm upwards, compress distances and are superb for creating stunning portraits.

ABOVE

A mirror carp held just above the water's surface creates a superb reflection. This shot is a powerful example of what a telephoto lens can do. This time, I used a 600mm lens to compress distance and render everything in front of and behind the fish to a dreamy blur. Telephoto lenses and wide apertures create stunning shots, lifting the subject out of its background. 600mm, 1/160th sec at f5.6, ISO100. Mounted.

400mm 2.8: what a lens this is! Huge and weighing the proverbial ton, you can't carry it very far and it cannot be used without some form of support. I love it, though. Though hardly a choice for the casual photographer, I always carry my 400mm when I can get the car close to the water.

The results are razor, razor sharp and its ability to blur background distractions makes for some high-impact photography. A lens like this is really only useful to pro's and anglers interested in action, wildlife and bird photography.

600mm f4: I ended up buying this lens off e-bay when I bid for the above long lens and this one at the same time, never thinking that I would win both auctions! It was my intention to sell one of them but I can't bear to part with either. The 600mm is truly wicked for long lens work, nature and action photography.

Phew! Now you know what I meant when I talked about photography being seriously addictive! Owning as many lenses as I do simply isn't necessary (though I'll admit it is fun!) It has taken me almost a decade of photography to build up my collection of kit but for most angling photography, one or just a handful of lenses will help you to take some great pictures. So what should you buy?

If restricted to just one lens, I would choose a medium zoom, probably in the range of 18-55mm on a standard DSLR body. Next, I'd buy a decent wide angle, something like 17-35mm on a full-frame sensor camera or 10-22mm for a regular DSLR before finally treating myself to a long zoom lens such as the 70-200mm or 75-300mm. While hunting round e-bay, I would consider picking up a 50mm prime for use when I want someone else to grab a catch shot for me. Finally, I'd purchase a nice macro lens to while away those hours when the fish aren't biting.

LENS
CHECKLIST

Portraits: (trophy shots): medium lenses around 50mm are the standard choice here. A long lens at 200mm or more can make for a good portrait shot if you want captor and fish to jump out from a blurred background whereas if you want to get angler, fish and some of the surroundings in you should use a wide angle.

Landscapes: usually best with a wide angle lens on a tripod. Wide angles pull in lots of the scene, offering excellent depth of field from foreground to background. They give a feeling of space. Medium length zooms are useful too, being wide enough to giving a feeling of space but not too wide. While some landscapes simply rock when shot ultra-wide, sometimes they can look to desolate. A medium telephoto can often deliver a better result, allowing you to crop out unwanted space. Some landscapes, such as a winding river or distant hills look great when shot on a long zoom, but remember that long lenses compress distances. A 10-22mm and 18-55mm lens for non-pro DSLR's or 16-35mm and 28-70mm are the pro equivalents.

Action: take your pick! Wide angles usually create more drama because the photographer is closer to the action, often getting splashed with water! Action shots from further away have a more focused, isolated feel, reducing the image to simpler, cleaner lines. The 10-22mm or 16-35 will take great wide angle action shots while at the longer end the 70-200mm fits the bill perfectly.

Macro: obviously you will need a macro lens for these but some decent results can be achieved with a long lens and a tripod to isolate detail from objects or scenes. A 50mm or 100mm Macro lens would be the standard choice.

Nature: long lenses rule supreme here. Wild birds and animals rarely let you get close to them. The minimum maximum focal length should be 200mm but 300 or 400 are better.

Knowing which to use lenses of different focal lengths is half of the battle. As a general rule, wide angle lenses offer a greater depth of field no matter what aperture and shutter speed you use while long lenses compress distances and deliver a shallower depth of field even when stopped down.

Ultimately, choosing the right lens and shooting at the right focal length is one of the qualities that helps sort the men out from the boys. A scene shot at 20mm might look rather uninviting but crash in on the same subject at 150mm, isolating key details and bingo, you have a great shot!

By the same token, there is always more than one way to shoot any subject. The great thing about photography is that you can interpret a subject from so many angles using different lenses and get totally different results. Mood, atmosphere and impact can vary greatly. Rarely do photographers interpret the same scene exactly the same way and long may it be that way.

Eventually, not only will you learn to 'see' photographs through your naked eyes you will eventually learn to 'see in lenses.' In other words, as you stand looking at a potential image, your eyes will be sub-consciously framing it at 16, 35, 50 and 100mm or more. Whilst you have simply 'looked' in the past, you must now 'see.' Just because something looks good to the naked eye does not mean it will make a great picture, no matter what lens you use. Some images just don't make good photographs but you will eventually learn to recognise them.

On the other hand, there will be scenes that don't look so good at a casual glance but look again and see. By using a 200mm you can pick out the silhouette of the bird on the fence post; the angler to your left is standing against a backdrop of shiny water; the reflection of those reeds in the water makes a great abstract; the sun will burst out from behind the clouds in a moment and swamp the scene in warm, glorious light...

You will also learn to use your lenses to their optimum. You will know, instinctively, that your 200mm will compress the distance between the most shrouded hills and deliver a peach of a shot; you will wait, with a favourite wide-angle lens fitted, for your mate to hook another fish so that you can wade into the shallow water in front of him, ready to nail a busting action shot; you will position your friend in that patch of warm light knowing that the trophy shot on your 50mm will sing when the fish's golden scales get lit-up...

BELOW
Great use of a wide-angle zoom lens adjusted to give just the right effect. The photographer has adopted a low position and concentrated on framing the shot. I set up the camera on manual settings, allowing friend, Mick Brown, to get a great shot of me bringing a fish to hand. 32mm, 1/100th sec, f11, ISO 200.

Chapter Four
TAKING GOOD
TROPHY SHOTS

There are certain basic techniques that will make you a better photographer even if you never switch the camera off auto. Later, we'll examine some of the basics of how photography works so that you can switch that auto function 'off' and venture into the world of creative angling photography. For the time being, though, we'll set aside the f-numbers and shutter speeds and concentrate on how to take a decent photograph that doesn't look blurred, wonky or cut your friends' heads off.

When we consider the basics of angling photography, in addition to the photographer, we should also give thought to the subject. Since basic angling photography refers to taking catch pictures, the person holding the fish and how he/she behaves is as important as the person holding the camera. Anglers who display fish properly always end up with better trophy shots than those awkward posers who are all fingers and thumbs...

Being familiar with how your camera works is very important. All cameras, even camera phones, come with an instruction booklet and you should read it. Learn about the different shooting modes and how to switch the flash on and off because flash is very important when taking catch photos.

You must also learn how to handle your camera: if you move, or your hands are shaking when you take the photo, the resulting image will either be badly framed, blurred or a combination of both. Grip the camera steadily and learn to stabilise it either by resting it on something or connecting it to tripod. Tripods are not strictly necessary for catch photos but they can help, especially when it is not you taking the photograph. For hand held photography, get into the habit of kneeling to take the shot. With your elbows crooked and resting on your knees you will stabilise the camera and drastically reduce camera shake - the benefit being sharper, crisper images. You will also find that kneeling, not standing up, results in better looking catch pictures since shooting from a low viewpoint tends to isolate the subject better from a cluttered background. Shots taken from above the angler will increase the risk of the subject merging in with the background and you will almost certainly frame your subject against mud or grass.

BELOW
The single-hand trophy pose is very effective with the smaller fish species. Two hands swamp the fish while one hand does not. A tricky one for the angler to master but the result is worth it.

clutter that has been left around the swim will also creep into the photo and this can be very distracting. The only time that I have found a shot like this to work well is when a fish is being returned to the water. This is because water is not cluttered and the high angle focuses the viewer's attention on the fish and its natural environment. Big fish can look particularly impressive when shot this way because the broadness of the fish (not seen when viewed side-on) is obvious.

For taking regular trophy or catch shots, with your elbows resting on your knees and the subject nicely framed, you should depress the camera shutter button slowly but positively and wait until you hear the shutter release noise before you remove your finger or the move the camera. This is a critical moment, especially with digital compacts and camera phones. These cheaper cameras often have an annoying delay between when you press the shutter button and when the photograph is taken. It is quite normal during these excessive delays for the photographer to move the camera while declaring 'I'm not sure that this has worked...' or something similar. A moment later you hear the sound of the shutter and the viewfinder displays an image of the sky, the ground or photographer's leg.

If you own a compact or DSLR type camera it is very important that you learn how to focus properly in auto mode. Most often, this is achieved by lightly depressing the shutter button and then, when focus is confirmed either by lights in the viewfinder or a 'bleep' the finger is pushed all the way down to take the picture.

Where you focus is very important too. The best results will be achieved by focusing on the fish's eye, not the angler. Some cameras allow you to focus and then shift the frame - a very useful facility. To do this, focus on the fish by semi-depressing the shutter button (flashing lights in the viewfinder and an audible 'beep' will usually accompany a successful focus) and with the button still semi-depressed, shift the frame until you have angler and fish clearly in shot.

Only when you are happy with the final frame should you push the button all the way down to release the shutter and take the picture. While this is one of the most important skills for you, the photographer to acquire, teaching a novice to focus shift is very difficult. Most compact cameras handle the situation quite well, actually, but DSLR's have more complex focusing systems and it is very common to get a shot with a pin sharp captor and a fish that is blurred. It helps enormously if you can hold the fish on the same plane as your body. To do this, kneel facing slightly sideways, with the fish the same distance from the camera as your face.

TOP

This trophy shot has been marred. The composition and exposure are superb but the presence of the rod growing out of my shoulder, the rod in the bottom left and the tree sapling are very distracting. Framing out the sapling and a simple tidy up of the scene would dramatically improve this image.

ABOVE

A high impact catch shot. Slightly cutting off the top of my head has not spoilt the image for this close crop. I would not normally advise this, but tilting one's head slightly makes the crop work.

This avoids the problem of the camera locking onto the person and rendering the fish out of focus. When friends or novices take catch shots for you, holding the fish an equal distance from the camera as your face is a good discipline to get into.

One of the biggest mistakes made in trophy photography is made by the subject not the photographer: holding the fish at arms length and offering it toward the camera not only distorts the fish and makes it look disproportionate, it also results in a shot that features the fish in-focus and the captor 'soft.' Whilst this 'wide angle' effect can occasionally look good it generally does not.

Some people do it because they believe that it makes the fish look bigger but trust me, serious anglers with experience of photography are never fooled. Better to hold the fish closer to your body and avoid the distortion effect...

Getting to know how to activate your camera's flash is another very important feature of catch or trophy photography. I cannot think of the last time that I took a trophy shot without fill-flash. Contrary to popular opinion (which tends to favour bright, sunny days), the best days for catch pictures are those soft, dull days when the light is diffused by cloud. In these conditions, exposures are very even, skin tones are perfect and the colours in the picture are beautifully saturated. A burst of fill flash adds some extra punch and sparkle to the picture and 'catch lights' in the subjects eyes (these are always good on portraits). On bright, sunny days, shadows and contrast are very, very harsh. Fill-flash helps to eliminate some of the harsh shadows caused by the bright sun such as cap shadows. Compact cameras and camera phones really struggle with harsh shadows in such conditions and usually fail to capture key detail. With DSLR's, the file sizes often capture detail that is not visible in the original exposure but can be dragged out in post-production using the recovery slider in the editing software. Nonetheless, fill-flash will improve every catch photo you take by filling in shadow areas and adding some extra punch.

BELOW
This is a prime example of distortion caused by using a wide-angle lens for trophy shots. The zander in the photograph was a double-figure fish but in the picture, it looks to be twice as big. The old phrase 'the camera never lies' is disproved by this shot. Wide-angle lenses can be used for trophy shots but their effects should be carefully controlled to avoid misleading images. 14mm optically corrected lens, 1/30th sec at f8, ISO 100, fill-flash.

Understanding the ISO settings on your camera and how to override them is also important. Most camera phones and compact cameras will set the ISO film speed automatically but it is sensible to shoot at the lowest ISO that you can. ISO is the old film speed standard. 100 is the standard film with speeds of 25, 50, 200 400, 800 and 1600 or more are available The higher the number the faster the film absorbs the light. What this meant, in practice, was that you could shoot twice as fast in the same light with 200 speed film as 100 and 4 times as fast with 400 as you could with ISO100. So why no use the fast film all the time you ask?

TOP

A cracking catch shot. Multiple features make this a great image: Firstly, the low viewpoint has created an interesting angle. Secondly, the fish is displayed beautifully and held at a slight angle. Thirdly, the use of a long or telephoto lens has reduced the background to a blur. Fourthly, the use of a relatively high f-number, in this case f8, has rendered both fish and captor pin-sharp. A medium aperture like f8 would have been pointless with a wide-angle lens because it would deliver too much depth of field. Finally, the use of just a hint of fill flash has put a sparkle in the captor's eyes emphasising his delight at the capture of such a beautiful fish.

MIDDLE

Captor Inga Holen cradles a beautiful, fresh salmon caught from Norway's Gaula river. The use of fill flash adds catch lights to the captor's eyes. Taking the photo from a slight angle helps to prevent the flash from bouncing directly back into the lens - an important consideration with silver fish.

BOTTOM

Mick Brown is a pro and a veteran of many photo shoots. Here, he shows how to hold a large, special fish. The cradling pose would not work with a small fish but with this big carp, illustrates that he is holding something special and cherished. Despite the dull weather conditions and washed-out sky, the low viewpoint adopted by the photographer makes fish and captor jump out from the rather uninspiring background. An aperture of f6.3 has kept all of the key detail sharp while the background is soft. The use of fill-flash captures the sparkle in Mick's eyes and adds extra punch to the shot.

ABOVE

Adrian Davey releases a rainbow trout caught in beautiful, early evening light. This shot demonstrates that quality of light can make the difference between a decent and a good image. Here a close crop has been used, cutting off the top of the angler's head but in this case, the composition works because the viewer's attention is drawn to the superb fish. A shallow depth of field has been achieved by using a wide aperture, effectively lifting trout and captor out of the background. A reflector has been deployed to reflect some of that fabulous warm light. 700mm lens, 1/250th sec at f5.6, ISO 50, fill-light via reflector.

RIGHT

Another way to display fish for a trophy shot. Welfare of the fish is paramount and the use of a rack, or in this case, a keep net, base helps to display and protect at the same time.

The answer is that the faster the film the more grain it would have and the less detail it would capture. Photographers always wanted to use the lowest ISO speed they could get away with because the slower films delivered sharper images, less grain and punchier colours. Compact cameras and DSLR's work the same way.

The ISO settings are the same as the old film speeds - the higher the ISO setting you use the faster the shutter speed but the worse the problem with grain (pixel detail). It is therefore advantageous, in decent light conditions to use a speed of ISO 100. In low light, at dusk, for example, 200 or 400 might be better. Modern ISO speed settings are delivering amazing results with digital. Some of the pictures on top DSLR's shot at ISO 1600 are nothing short of magnificent in terms of detail and general image quality. Nonetheless, a photo taken at a low ISO setting will always have better colour saturation and less grain or digital noise.

At first, you will be happy to accept the ISO setting that your compact camera

sets for you. If you own a DSLR you have the option to set it manually and as your technique improves you will want to do this. In daylight, set it to 100 or 160 for catch shots and in the dark use 200 or 400. These are good starting out points.

Compact camera users might like to experiment with setting different ISO's and comparing the results when they blow the photos up on a screen or make a print. This really is the acid test because photos that look good on the LCD screen on the back of your camera don't always look good when blown up. Shots taken on lower ISO's will have less 'grain,' punchier colours and a sharper look. And with digital cameras you will not really be able to see how good the shots are until you blow them up to 100% size on your computer screen.

At this resolution, any digital noise present will become visible as a distinct grain and will also be visible in the colour saturation. Modern software for post-production features noise reduction options and you should become familiar with how best to operate these facilities on your chosen software.

ABOVE
A prime example of a great fish that deserves a better photograph. The horizon slopes; the background is totally distracting and the image is generally cluttered. The overall effect is that an impressive fish, the main subject, is slightly lost among the chaos.

LEFT
The way in which the angler displays the fish can dramatically affect the mood of an image. In this case, Eric Hope cradles the fish gently above the water, conveying a sense of how precious the wild brown trout is.

One of the most important things to do with catch photography is to prepare. This preparation should take place before you fish (by briefing fishing friends about how to use your camera) and immediately prior to the trophy shot being taken. While you get the camera ready, for example, keep the fish in the water in a landing net. You can either ask a friend to hold the net for you or stake it out in some way but make sure that the fish is supported in a natural position with plenty of water around it.

The fish should be oriented in its natural, head-facing-the-current position and it should look comfortable – avoid the danger of the mesh of the net being tightly wrapped around the fish. Done correctly, this procedure keeps the fish safe while you switch on the camera and set it up. Next, scout the surrounding area for a decent location. You are looking for a position where the light is even. On dull, cloudy days this is not so much of a consideration but if it is sunny, choose a spot that the sun is shining on and make sure that the subject will be facing the sun. Later we will look at how to take

images into the sun with a technique known as 'rim lighting' but this is quite tricky and best left alone until you are really keen. Always check what will be behind the subject. Grasses, reeds and dense bushes with short branches are fine - water is good too. Try to avoid fences, large trees and buildings. Structures like these have a habit of 'growing' out of the subjects head or shoulder and this is one of the cardinal sins of photography.

Also check the background for anything that might be distracting - white or yellow, bright blue, orange and red are particularly bad. Many a good shot has been ruined by a plastic bag, lifebelt or other bright-coloured object in the background. Indeed, you should make a point of clearing the photographic area of clutter and this includes nets, tackle boxes, rod sleeves, bait bags and rod sleeves. The purpose of this is to remove anything that might distract the viewer's attention from the main image of captor with fish. Believe me, any clutter left in the shot can and will stand out - once spotted it will draw your eye like a magnet.

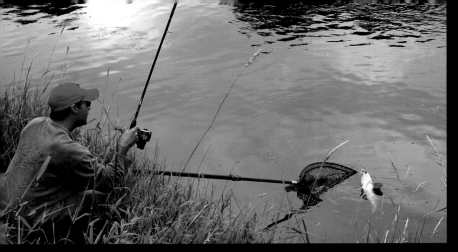

position that you will adopt, pretending to hold the fish. You can then focus, and adjust the camera. Take a shot and check it. When happy, mark yours and your friend's positions (small sticks placed in line with your toes are perfect). This pre-work will avoid unnecessary mistakes such as chopped off heads, objects growing out of the subject's head, out-of-focus photographs etc.,

You should also give thought to the ground over which the captor will hold the fish while the picture is taken. Soft grass or water is best. Some types of angling involve the use of unhooking mats as standard equipment and these special mats that protect the fish from damage can be deployed even on hard banks. The main point is not to allow the fish to come into contact with rough, abrasive or hard surfaces...

Your next task is to set the camera up by switching it on and setting it to 'auto'

when a friend is taking the shot or by manually setting the aperture, shutter speed and ISO number if you are more knowledgeable. A camera mounted on a tripod is always a good idea if you have time.

Firing a test shot or two is always a good idea, whether doing self-photography or using a friend. That way you can check the framing, the exposure and the focus. When enlisting the help of a friend. Choose your photography position and kneel down. Get your friend to pose in the

ABOVE
This shot illustrates how distracting bright objects can be in an image. The red hat draws attention away from the main subject, the fish being netted.

BELOW
A very nice trophy shot of me with an amberjack from Costa Rica. The low angle and holding the fish with its head toward the camera add impact and draw attention to the striking business end of the fish. The red hat provides a splash of colour and is not distracting because it is part of the main subject.

CHECKLIST

1. Choose a location with even lighting (not under the dappled shade of a tree for example.

2. Pose with the fish facing the light, not away from it.

3. Check the background to avoid clutter such as signs, buckets, lifebelts or objects of bright colour. If you cannot remove them, shift position. Also remove any bank side clutter such as fishing gear, bags, etc.,

4. Check the backdrop and ground. The captor should not have branches or other objects growing out of their heads. If this is unavoidable, shooting with a long lens and a shallow depth-of-field will help to isolate the captor. Check the ground - is it soft enough (grasses are best) to protect the fish if dropped or lowered to the ground? If not, use an unhooking mat or something padded to protect the fish. A bucket of water next to captor and fish (if you have time and opportunity) is a good idea. Splashing water on the fish immediately prior to taking the shot will keep it in good condition and the resulting shot will have extra 'zing.'

5. The photographer should kneel down to take the shot and generally so should the captor. These low angles will isolate the subject for the background and look more natural. Kneeling with the fish above the water is even better. A camera on a low-angle tripod is a good idea.

6. The photographer should rest elbows on knees and check the frame. Alternatively, the camera should be on a tripod. The best trophy shots will see the captor and fish fill as much of the frame as possible. Holding the camera portrait style (upright) is usually best. Make sure that the subject is in the frame (don't cut off the head) and that the fish is also fully framed (tail and fins). Do not, however, make the mistake of allowing too much space around the subject. These shots, where the captor and fish appear miles away are a waste of time. Get as close as possible without cutting off extremities and fill the frame with captor and fish. At this stage, this is the 'rehearsal frame' and the one that the camera will ultimately capture.

7. Check that the flash is turned on.

8. The captor should look pleased, excited or relaxed. Avoid the 'James Dean' look - it is anorak! The captor should also wet their hands - this is much kinder to the fish and avoids damage to the protective mucus that covers the fish's body.

9. The photographer should focus. This might have been done manually before the shot or, more usually by autofocus. In this case, half-depress the shutter button whilst focusing on the fish's eye. When the focus locks on (usually accompanied by some flashing lights in the viewfinder and a 'beep'), keep the firing button half-depressed and shift the frame back to the one rehearsed earlier.

10. When happy with focus and frame, press the shutter button all the way.

11. Check image to ensure that it is sharp and with good framing.

12. Avoid keeping the fish out of the water for more than a few shots. If you need more time, return the fish to the water in a net and give it good recovery time between shots.

For some, angling has always been a 'lone' pursuit and even for those of us whom crave company, there are occasions when we fish alone. This does not necessarily mean that we can't take good 'catch' pictures but it does make things more difficult. Preparation and having the right equipment is the key to self-portrait angling photography. A Norwegian fly-fishing friend, Hans Erik, is a master of self-portraiture. He spends a great deal of time fishing alone and with his compact camera he takes great trophy shots.

He achieves this by being thoroughly acquainted with how the camera works and how to use it. Being a fly fisher, he often fishes in remote and hostile places but working knowledge of his camera means that he takes good pictures wherever he goes. A lightweight tripod is also a permanent piece of equipment - he takes it with him, collapsed in a backpack wherever he goes. Using simple equipment he has managed to obtain great film footage and stills when fishing alone in hostile environments.

There is certain equipment that is absolutely vital for self-portraiture with fish. Item number one is a landing net - this is used to retain the fish while the camera is set-up. Deepish, steady water close to the bank should be sought out and the net positioned so that the fish is held upright with its head facing any current. To support the net, a stick or bank stick should be pushed into the gap between mesh and frame. This prevents the fish bolting away with the net. Other sticks can be used, if necessary to prevent the mesh from sticking too closely to the fish's body. The net retains the fish while the camera is set-up.

Item number two is a tripod. Anglers whom fish largely static will probably favour a regular tripod while those whom like to rove should carry one of the lightweight specialist pods such as the Joby Gorillapod or the Trek-tech' by Optera. Whilst unsuitable for serious tripod work, these lightweight, compact pods are just the job for a quick 'grab' shot. They feature flexible legs that can be used to grip onto fence posts, branches and bridge structures too.

Item number three is some form of delayed timer on your camera or a remote release. Most serious anglers combine both but self-timers on their own are fine at a push. The best self-timers will have a delay of ten seconds or more. Anything shorter makes catch pictures impossible.

To frame and focus the picture is the next task. To do so you need to make sure that your head is not going to be cut off and that the whole of the fish is in the shot. On the other hand, you want to fill the frame and not 'zoom out',

How to Make a Self Portrait Frame

1. Kneel in position and place a stick in the ground directly in line with where you will hold the fish. The positioning of the stick is critical - it must be the same distance from the camera as the flank of the fish will be. To establish this position, make a fake pose, pretending to hold the fish.

2. The height of the stick should be adjusted to the top of your head. While still kneeling, break it off just above the top of your head. This will ensure that you now have a focal point and your head will be in the shot.

3. Next, deal with the edges of frame. Place a further twig either side of you where you want frame to cut off. Allow around a foot (30cm) of extra room either side of where you want the frame to cut off.

4. Next, break off these twigs so that they are at a lower height (around 30cm) than the fish's belly will be. This marks the lower edge of the frame. Once again, making the false 'pose' will help because the sticks can be broken below where you expect the fish's belly to be with accuracy.

5. Now that you have the top and the edges of the frame marked, you can position your camera on the tripod and frame correctly. The middle stick should be in the centre of the frame. Have the top of the middle stick just inside the top of the frame and the two 'side' sticks just about cropped out.

In other words, you should frame just inside the two outer sticks so that they do not appear in the picture (but only just). Also make sure that the lower edge of the frame is level with the tops of these sticks. This way, everything that should be in the picture will be in the picture.

6. Focus the camera on the stick and put it back to manual focus to prevent the lens from 'hunting' for a focal point when you take the shot. Focusing on the stick is critical, this being the level where the fish's flank will be. With compact cameras, locking off to manual focus will not be possible so the camera will have to be left on autofocus.

7. Select the picture taking mode. Auto is most people's choice and it usually works except in low light when shallow depth of field (the captor is not in focus) can be a problem.

Manual is good, usually at f5.6 with the appropriate shutter speed but for those unfamiliar with manual settings, set the camera at AV (Aperture priority) 5.6 or 'Portrait' mode. Get the fish and activate the timer. Set it to take several pictures if possible. Most self-release timers will allow you to do this. If it is dark you will need to turn the flash on.

8. Get the fish (still in the net) and get into the pre-rehearsed position. Knock the middle forward so that it is low to ground and no longer in the shot.

9. Take the fish out of the net and pose. You may miss the first shot, but don't panic, the camera will carry on taking shots if you have set it up correctly.

10. After three or four shots, place the fish back in the net, rest it in the water and check your shots.

SELF-PHOTOGRAPHY EQUIPMENT
CHECKLIST

1. Camera with self-timer of at least ten seconds.

2. Remote release or self-timer that allows you to take continuous shots

3. Landing net

4. Head torch (if night fishing)

5. Sticks or bank sticks

6. For static fishing locations: unhooking mat and bucket (to fill with water and wet fish between shots).

Using these techniques it is possible to take good trophy shots in almost any location. The techniques described can even be used to take catch pictures in the dark but if you are night fishing it pays to prepare a photographic area before you start fishing and in the daylight. Mount the camera on the tripod, use the sticks to make the frame and have everything ready and pre-focused. If you arrive in the dark, set the 'studio' up and use a head torch to focus and set the edges of the frame.

When you have caught a fish it is simply a matter of returning to the camera position, switching the camera on and posing for the shots. Indeed, preparing the frame before you fish is always a good idea unless you are covering large distances. If it is possible to return the fish to the camera location without distressing it, the 'studio on the bank' is a great idea. Of course, you will need to take care that the tripod is stabilised and not liable to blow over. As a precaution, covering the camera with a rain protector can also save a lot of heartache.

Whilst this might seem to be a lot of preparation, especially when fishing in wilderness locations, it is invariably worth it if you catch the fish of a lifetime.

Finally, a few words about fish care. No trophy shot should be attempted if the fish cannot be photographed safely and returned to the water in mint condition. You will occasionally encounter circumstances where it is simply impossible to take a good trophy shot and as an angler and conservationist you have to accept this. In most circumstances, however, preparation and forward thinking can ensure that a good photograph can be taken without detriment to the fish. If practical and especially when fishing in 'static' angling locations, the most important accessories are an unhooking mat, a landing net and a bucket of water. Never keep the fish out of the water for longer than a few shots and always keep it low to the ground, either over the mat, over water, or over soft vegetation. Above all, get to know how your camera works and learn to operate it intuitively and in the dark.

LEFT
Matt with barbel; this shot was taken using a compact camera with built-in flash. A self-taken shot, Matt used the techniques described to achieve a decent result when fishing on his own in the middle of a cold autumn night.

ABOVE
The ultimate sailfish release by Peter Collingsworth in Costa Rica. This type of catch photography elevates the trophy shot to a new level!

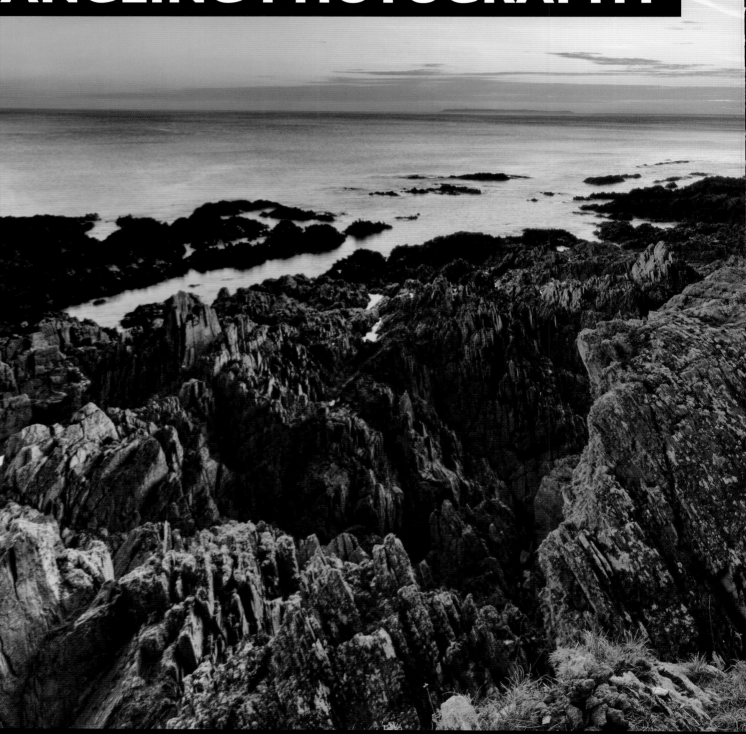

Chapter Five

THE KEYS TO CREATIVE ANGLING PHOTOGRAPHY

M ost anglers will rarely venture beyond 'grip and grin' photography. Perhaps they might snap the odd fishing scene with a compact or camera phone but that is about the limit of their aspirations. With the widespread availability of digital SLR cameras, however, more of us are becoming creative with our angling photography. This is especially true of anglers whom write fishing features for magazines or contribute to websites. For some, taking better angling pictures is a joy in itself. Either way, there is only so much you can achieve with a camera set to auto mode.

The advent of the video blog and the availability of cheap DSLR cameras that deliver professional results means that many anglers in the future will have the equipment to take great stills and movies. However, there will always be a difference between amateur and professional, albeit that the gap is narrower than it used to be.

In a nutshell, you start to become a creative angling photographer when you switch the camera auto modes off. It is a huge leap of faith and one that is bound to result in some failures and mistakes but in these times of modern digital cameras it is possible to go on a much faster learning curve than ever it was in the days when everyone used film. You can instantly review tweaks made to apertures, exposures, flash settings and framing.

I have seen numerous features in angling magazines shot by contributors or editors with the camera set on 'auto.' Invariably, the results are disappointing. Lack of control of depth of field, poor framing, poor exposures, burnt-out-skies and pictures that lack impact are the hallmarks of this type of work. Of course, modern cameras are getting better all the time but they cannot compensate for a lack of knowledge of photography. Professional photographers, like my friends Mick Rouse and Lloyd Rogers (Bauer publishing), are now a rare breed.

BELOW

Carp angler Mark Hutchinson launches a trademark power cast. The framing is perfect here with the rod filling the empty space at the top of the frame. A fast shutter speed has captured the moment of the cast and the curve of the rod. A slight touch of motion blur on the rod adds a sense of movement. The red shirt, potentially distracting in this case draws attention to the main subject and adds colour to the image.

let their work is outstanding. The arrival of the digital era has not meant that an amateur or magazine editor can hope to photograph an angling feature as they would. These guys understand how to frame pictures, use the different lenses they own to optimum effect, control depth of field and exposure. If they were asked to photograph a fishing feature at the same time as an amateur using the camera on auto mode, the features would have a totally different feel because of the quality of the photography.

Photographers like Mick and Lloyd have the knowledge and experience to convey in pictures what it was like to be on the bank that day. They can create mood, drama or impact. They will be ready to capture spontaneous moments, safe in the knowledge that they know what shutter speed and aperture to set to capture a rod fully-flexed during a cast or a leaping fish. Their knowledge of how flash works will help them to create pictures with added mood and drama. In short, their knowledge of photography techniques will always out-perform even the best camera set to 'auto.'

It is also noticeable that great photographers have a signature to their work. It has a certain look and feel whilst features shot by 'auto mode' photographers lack personality.

In short, the real key to taking great angling photographs is to study and understand the basics of photography. The interesting thing is that they have not changed, even with the advent of digital cameras. About the only difference between photography with film and digital is that film grain has been replaced by 'digital noise' and high ISO performance (shooting in low light) is improving all the time. Arguably the arrival of HDR (High Dynamic Range) photography is the biggest leap forward over the film days. HDR works by combining several images taken at different exposures to create a composite image that can capture a range of tone and detail (especially in the shadows and highlights) that a single exposure simply cannot do (at the moment!) Yet, true HDR photography will only work properly if the scene being photographed

is static and lacking any significant movement, so it has its limitations. We will look at HDR later.

The basic building blocks of any form of photography are framing, controlling and using quality of light, ISO (film speeds), apertures and shutter speeds. This has always been the case and for the foreseeable future these are still the keys to being able to 'interpret' scenes and take photographs as opposed to 'snaps.'

We will deal with framing and light control in the next chapter but for the time being lets deal with the grunt work – apertures, shutter speeds and IS0's – the building blocks. Think of apertures as being the amount of light, shutter speeds as being the amount of time the light is allowed to pass and ISO as the speed at which it travels. The three are interconnected and control the amount and intensity of light that reach the camera's sensor. Only when the balance is right do we get a properly exposed image

ABOVE

A Costa Rican sailfish emerges from the wate displaying vibrant colours. A fast shutter speed 1/2000th of a second and a wide apertur capture the moment

I do not intend to go into the mechanics of how cameras work because most of you, I suspect do not want to study camera theory: you are simply interested in the end result. What you must understand, however, is that when you depress the shutter button, what the sensor on your camera records will depend on the shutter speed and how wide the aperture opens up. It will also depend on the speed of the light (ISO) entering the camera. This effect is created by a shutter located inside the lens. This is formed by a series of overlapping blades that when open allow light to pass into the camera: the mirror inside the camera flips up and the sensor records the image. The length of time the blades are open and the size of the hole that opens up control the image that is recorded onto the camera's sensor. Think of this mechanism as being like the iris in your eye. It too opens and closes to control the passage of light. Shutter speeds are the length of time that the camera's 'iris' is open for (usually in fractions of a second but possibly for several seconds, minutes or even hours) and the aperture is how wide the blades in the 'iris' are

open. The amount of light is partially dictated by how long the shutter is open for and also by the size of the 'hole' that opens up in the lens blades when the shutter mechanism is fired. A narrow hole will result in a long depth of field (whereby everything from foreground to background is sharp and in focus) whilst a wide aperture or hole will result in a shallow depth of field where only the focal point are a short area in front of and behind it will be in focus and the rest of the scene will be blurred.

I recently read a good explanation of how apertures work on the internet ('Answers.com'). It goes as follows:

'The aperture is like the iris of the eye. When the aperture is very small, you will get a sharper focus and more depth of field-- near and far things in the scene will tend to be sharper. This is because the smaller circle is cutting down on the "confusion" caused by the countless overlapping circles of light being focused on the film or other light sensitive surface in the camera.

LEFT
A bull dorado leaps from the water displaying bright colours. A fast shutter speed of 1/2000th of a second freezes the action.

BELOW
A long lens (100mm) set at f5.6 delivers a shallow depth of field. In this image, only the head of the orange lure is in sharp focus, and the reel at the rear of the image is reduced to an impressionistic blur. 100mm, 1/20th sec at f5.6, ISO 100.

The down side is that because the iris is smaller, less light is getting in, and you need a longer exposure to get a good image. When the aperture is larger, you can get a good image with a faster exposure, but sharpness and depth of field may suffer a little. The "circles of confusion" are larger, because the aperture is larger...'

This is a very good explanation and one that suits our purposes perfectly. The end result of the amount of light that passes onto the cameras sensor and the amount of time that the sensor is exposed to the light creates the exposure. Photographers refer to exposures as being 'perfectly,' 'under' or 'over' exposed. In other words, an image can be just right, too dark or too bright. Sometimes we seek to create images that are deliberately over or under-exposed but this is usually to draw attention to a particular part of an image and it is more usual to aim for correct exposure, this being the exposure closest to that seen by the human eye. The depth of field is also controlled by the shutter reflex – the size of the aperture will dictate whether the whole scene is sharp and in focus, a proportion of it or a fraction of it. Shallow depth of field is used to draw attention to key parts of the scene (catch photos for example) while longer depths of field are typically used in landscape photography.

RIGHT
This shot of a group of crabs that emerged from burrows on a beach in Mozambique shows the power of depth f field. Only one of the crabs, the second in line, is in focus. The crab in the foreground is slightly blurred while the rest of the group are reduced to a vague impression. The effect is to focus attention on the crab furthest to the left. To achieve this effect I used a wide aperture and a telephoto lens (to compress distance). Lens 400mm, 1/320th sec at f4, ISO 200.

t is the combination of aperture and shutter speed that create exposure. If we use a narrow aperture to render everything from foreground to background in focus, we must use a longer shutter speed (the amount of time the shutter is open) to allow enough light through to create a good exposure. If, on the other hand we use a wide aperture and create a very shallow depth of field, the shutter will only have to be open for a brief time to create a good exposure.

The relationship between aperture and shutter speed is what creates an exposure: the wider the aperture the shorter the exposure and vice-versa. The amount of time that the shutter will need to be open to create a good exposure is affected, of course, by the amount of light. The shutter will need to be open longer on a dull day, for example than on a bright day to create the same exposure. The device

that tells us how much light is available and what will create a good exposure for the chosen aperture is the camera's built-in light meter. As a general rule, portraiture relies on wide apertures with shallow depth of field while landscapes and scenes rely on narrow apertures and infinite depth of field.

To recap and to paint a practical example, let us imagine that we are photographing an angler standing on the bank next to a winding river. He is standing several meters away and appears as perhaps 10% of the image, the rest being the winding river, the grass, rocks, trees and sky. If we want the whole scene, from front to back, in focus, including the fisherman, the river, the sky and distant tree line, we set a narrow aperture (between f11 and f22). If we want to isolate the fisherman from his background and reduce the rest of the scene to an abstract blur, we choose a wide

aperture (say, f2.8 or f4). After setting the aperture, we rely on the camera's meter to tell us how long the exposure should be. At F16 it might be as long as 1/30th of a second (this will depend on how much light is present). In the same light conditions, a shutter speed of 1/1000th of a second at f2.8 will be right.

The size of the aperture is designated by what are known as 'f-stops.' The increments of the stops are as follows: 2.8, 5.6, 8, 11, 16 and 22. There are some more extreme stops such as f1 and f32 but these have little practical use in angling photography. The rule is that the lower the f-number the shallower the depth of field and vice-versa. The gap between f5.6 and f8 is a stop. The gap between f8 and 11 is a stop also. F6.3 and f7.1 are one third and two thirds of a stop above f5.6. A further one third of a stop takes it up to the next full stop – f8.

RIGHT

Fish don't have to be huge to make great pictures. This grilse caught in August from the Gaula in Norway makes a beautiful picture. A relatively wide-angle lens has kept most of the background in focus because when I set up this shot, I felt that the scenery was an important part of the story. Despite the fact that it was a bright day with lots of contrast, a reflector was used in place of fill-flash to fill in the shadows. 22mm, 1/100th sec, f6.3 ISO 200.

BELOW

Ed Brown casts a beautiful loop on a lake in the remote Innerdalen area of central Norway. This image shows the power of using a long lens and its ability to 'pull' the subject away from the background. The line is beautifully contrasted against the dark canopy of trees and rocks on the far side of the lake, accentuating the beauty of the cast. 200mm lens, 1/750th sec at f4, ISO 200.

ABOVE

The sunsets on lake Mjosa, Norway are to die for. In the early part of the summer, it never gets truly dark and after the sun has set, the twilight seems to last forever. I wanted to capture the anticipation that goes hand in hand with fishing the lake on a calm evening when the sky is painted with brilliant colours. For this image, I exposed for the sky in an attempt to retain the fabulous sunset colours and had to use fill flash to light Mick and the rear of the boat. The a of a shot like this is to use just enough flash to balan the exposure and not overwhelm the sky by over blowing the front of the image. This takes som experimentation with the flashgun set to manual an a diffuser fitted. In this case, I eventually opted t bounce the flash off the white sides of the boat t create a softer, more natural fill light. 28mm, 1/90t sec at f16, ISO 100, bounced fill flash.

F-Stops and Depth of Field – a Brief Guide

F2.8 – is a very shallow depth of field. Used with catch photos, the subject's face and the fish will both need to be the same distance from the camera for both to appear in focus.

F4 –gives slightly more depth of field but still shallow.

F5.6 – is a good depth of field for catch photos. Both the subject and the fish will be in focus but the background will be largely out of focus.

F8 –is a medium depth of field. Now objects in front of the captor and his trophy are coming into focus but not at extreme range.

F11 – almost everything except the most distant objects are in focus.

F16 – sharpness is achieved from foreground to background.

F22 – this produces focus in all parts of the scene but this aperture offers very few advantages over f16 and can also cause some image distortion.

Whilst the above rules hold good for most camera lenses, there's an element of distortion in some cases when using lenses at the extremes of focal range. For example, by 16-35mm Canon f2.8 lens has an almost Infinite depth of field even at f4 or F5.6 For this reason, it makes a poor portrait lens. Conversely, lenses with long focal lengths tend to compress distances and as such are used less frequently in landscape photography than wide angle lenses.

Calculating Exposure – the relationship between Aperture and Shutter Speed

Given the same amount of light on any given day, the relationship between shutter speed and aperture is easy to calculate once we have achieved a good exposure at one aperture. Let us assume that we have worked out that at f2.8 the correct shutter speed is 1500th of a second. The rest of the exposures can be worked out by halving the shutter speed for each full stop.

F2.8 – 1/500th
F4 – 1/250th
F5.6 – 1/125th
F8 – 1/60th
F11 – 1/30th
F16 – 1/15th

Also bear in mid the 'sunny 16' rule. I assumes that in strong light, an exposure o 1/125th of a second is correct for F16 at iso 100. Understanding this rule will help us t make a good stab at an exposure with any aperture selected.

By understanding this relationship, we can work out the correct shutter speed if we change aperture. It is also obvious that we need to use a tripod on occasions, especiall with narrow apertures designed to increas depth of field. As a general rule, it is only possible to hand hold a lens at its foca length expressed in hundredths of a second In other words, a 200mm lens cannot be hand held safely without getting camera shake (and thus blur or soft focus in th image) at less than 1/250th of a second. A wide angle lens, such as a 14mm, or the other hand can be hand held a shutter speeds down to 1/20th of a second without camera shake by experienced photographers.

When considering which aperture to set we must take into account not only whether we want a shallow depth of field but also how different lenses will portray scenes at the same aperture. Long lenses, above 100mm tend to compress distance and are designed to isolate subjects from backgrounds. With my 400mm lens set at f8 the depth of field still appears limited and yet with wide angle lenses, even low f numbers (wide apertures such as f4 there is a much greater depth o field. With my 14mm lens set at f4, fo example, almost the whole scene appears in focus provided I am not too close to the foreground object.

LEFT

Dave Kelbrick works a top water lure for pike in the lily pads. The low angle makes this shot, and i is a strong composition. The lure is the key subjec but there are several other subjects of interest in this shot including the boat, lily pads, angler, and moody sky. A shallow depth of field has been used by using a wide aperture, drawing attention to the lure and the lily pads.

BELOW

This image of Jens Christiansen casting from a waterfall benefits from strong composition and the use of a wide aperture to lift the subject away from the background. The cascade of water zigzagging among the rocks and the central placement of the angler balances the image - subjects often look better when placed off centre - a case when breaking the classic rules of composition worked. 400mm lens, 1/350th sec at f2.8, ISO 100.

Understanding how different lenses affect apparent depth of field is very important and has a large bearing on the final image. This is best achieved by firing test shots with your different lenses of the same scenes and comparing the depths of field. A nice way to do this is to set up by a river. Frame the shot with the river going from corner to corner as much as possible. Take shots with different lenses at different apertures and compare the results. Is the river in focus from front to back or is it more in focus at the front of the frame? How about trees – those close and further away from the camera? How about grasses or rocks near to the camera position? Compare fence lines. Indeed, shooting along fence lines and looking at how many posts are in focus depending on the aperture set is a great way to test the qualities of various lenses.

Setting the aperture to control the depth of field and consequently which parts of the image are in focus is the first decision you need to make after deciding the frame. Next, you will need to select a shutter speed to produce a good exposure. There are occasions, of course, when we deliberately under expose an image – a silhouette being a great example – but more often than not we want a correctly exposed image. To achieve this we need to use a meter that measures the amount of ambient or artificial light. More often than not this is the camera's built-in meter but some photographers use dedicated light meters if the light is tricky to measure.

For most people, however, the camera's light meter is the method of choice. Built-in light meters are getting better

all the time and they are very reliable except in certain circumstances. Extreme shadow or brightness in parts of a scene cause problems and fool camera meters into making the wrong exposure. The camera cannot create exposures that capture all details when there are excessively dark or bright portions of the frame – it can expose for the highlights, the mid-tones or the shadows but not all three.

Indeed, all exposures carry some compromise because they expose for what the camera's meter believes to be the dominant part of the scene. Actually, this is where HDR imaging comes in (see later) and it is also my belief that cameras will continue to improve the amount of detail they can capture in extremes of light. Currently we use post-processing software to 'bring back' excessive dark or light portions of the scene but we are getting closer to the day when the camera will do this during capture.

I digress. The light meter works by measuring the amount of light reflected back off objects in the frame. Because our eyes automatically adjust to extremes of light (the iris expands and contracts according to how much light hits it) the camera tries to arrange an exposure that most closely mimics how the eye would portray the scene. To do this it tries to render the scene according to a particular shade of grey that is considered to be the closest to the way the human eye sees. In the old days, photographers used 'grey cards' that had a shade of grey rated at 18% as a target. They were held in the light that fell on the subject and a meter reading was taken off the grey card (some photographers still use the technique and it is very accurate).

Inevitably, on all but the dullest of days when light is almost even across the whole scene, there will be extremes that the camera's meter can read or ignore. How much it allows these bright and dark portions to affect its calculation of exposure can be controlled. Every decent DSLR has a meter that can operate on spot, centre-weighted or evaluative metering. You should learn how to activate these different metering modes and how to use them.

Metering Modes

Spot – evaluates a small of the light falling on the image in the centre of the frame. This is very useful when you want just the focal point of the image to be correctly exposed

Centre Weighted – considers all the light in the scene but gives more importance to the light on the object in the centre.

Evaluative – the meter assesses the whole scene and tries to come up with the correct exposure taking into account all of the extremes

Reading this, you might wonder why to bother with anything other than evaluative, since this achieves the best compromise. Personally, I rarely use centre weighted, but I do use the camera's spot meter a lot – especially when the scene is filled with subjects of different brightness. A typical scene might include water (which can appear shiny or dark), trees, sky and grass. Almost all will give different readings if you point the lens at them (and this is the difficulty that evaluative metering attempts to overcome).

No matter how good the meter is, however, these subjects will be competing with each other to dominate the exposure gives. By spot metering off something of what I consider to be medium reflectance I usually get a good exposure.

ABOVE
Classic shallow depth of field stuff.

typically, I will hold the back of my hand in front of the camera (I am quite dark skinned) and meter off it. It is usually spot on! Alternatively, if you have very pale or dark skin, try metering on the most neutral-looking part of the sky (but not into the sun), a cloud, a medium grey rock or something else of a medium shade.

For many, the answer is to simply point the camera, let it work everything out and take the photograph. Most times, with exposures, the camera will do a good job. You can overcome these small discrepancies by learning to use the camera's bracketing mode. This allows you to take three exposures in a row – one correct, one under and one over exposed. You can set the amount of under and over exposure. Almost always, one of them is bound to be correct.

Sometimes however, you need to know how to get yourself out of trouble. Imagine a black cat in a coal hole or a white cat on a snow field. In both cases, when the meter takes its reading, it will come up with a shutter speed that will render the image that neutral shade of grey that the eye sees in. Yet, snow is not grey and nor is the cat. Coal is black. The answer in these tricky extremes of brightness is to take a meter reading and then deliberately override what the camera tells you by two stops. In the case of the snow it will try to darken it so for snow to appear white we open up by two stops. With coal, it will lighten it to make it grey so we close down by two stops. Some compact cameras now have 'snow modes.' These work simply by metering the scene and opening up by 2 f-stops to keep the snow white. The result will be that snow looks white and coal looks black. Although these are extremes, when harsh extremes of light are present in scene it is wise to bracket by up to one and a half stops (this means taking exposures above and below the shutter speed given by the meter).

The easiest way to test how exposures can be fooled is at sunset. If you want to expose a silhouette, position the subject against the sky and set the cameras meter mode to evaluative (it will be dominated by the light from the sky). It is retaining detail in the sky that becomes the meter's priority and so it advises us to use an exposure to retain detail and colour in the sky. The result is a beautiful sky with saturated colours and a subjects (maybe a person, an animal, a fishing rod or whatever) that is rendered black.

Your camera's AV mode is the first port of call when you decide to switch off auto. AV is Aperture Priority. You set the aperture of your choice and the camera' meter works out the correct exposure time for that aperture. By using exposure bracketing you can iron out any mistakes made by the meter except in the extreme circumstances. Under expose and over expose by a stop on your bracketing sequence and you will not go far wrong. If you are taking pictures in the extremes, try using exposure compensation – this feature allows you to adjust the exposure by as much or as little as you want and still shoot in AV mode.

Finally we come to ISO. This was the number used to designate the speed of film and whilst modern DSLR's do not use film their sensors are designed to react pretty much the same way as film did to quality of light. In the old days, ISO 100 or ISO 200 were the standard film speeds. Films were available as low as ISO 25 but these were specialised films designed for super saturation of colour when shooting on tripods. The rule is simple – the lower the ISO the sharper the image, the punchier the colours and the better the contrast. Nonetheless, quality comes at a price. These lower ISO's were slow films and needed good light for hand holding. Consequently, in low light, films of ISO 200, 400, 800 and even 1600 were used. These were faster, giving faster shutter speeds at the same aperture than lower ISO's but the result was more washed out colours, more grain (visible dots in the picture) and poorer contrast.

A digital SLR sensor works in the same way. If you set a low ISO you get great results but in poor light the shutter speeds will be very slow. The lower the ISO setting, the greater the detail it captures and the less digital noise appear on the image. The colours are bolder and the image looks sharper. Digital noise is ugly and takes the form of harsh 'pixels' that lack proper colour and definition. Digital noise is only really a problem when the image is seen at high resolution but nonetheless it is there and the amount of it is dictated by how high or low the ISO setting is.

BELOW
A slow shutter speed of several seconds makes this swiftly flowing mountain stream a dreamy blur. Shots like this require cooperation between photographer and angler. In this shot, my fishing pal, Ed Brown, displays infinite patience by remaining still for the duration of the exposure. Any slight movement will reduce him to a blur and ruin the image. If you are serious about angling photography, having patient friends is a must! The sky on this occasion was rather washed out and the use a graduated ND filter has helped to preserve some detail.

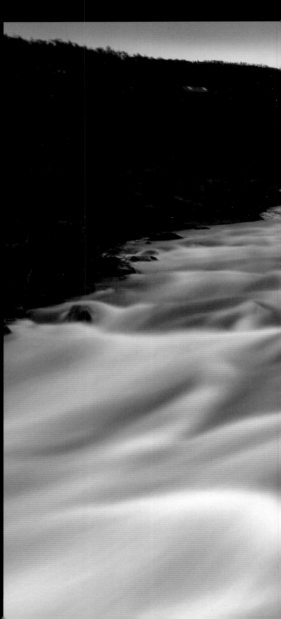

Nonetheless, the performance of modern digital cameras at higher ISO's has surpassed anything that even the best high ISO films could deliver. Some modern DSLR's come with ISO settings from L (usually ISO 50) to H (ISO 100000!) This makes it possible to take hand held shots in almost complete darkness! Having tried out this technology, I must say that I am happiest at L, happy at 100 to 200, fairly happy at 8OO, comfortable at 1000 and loath to go above this ISO setting because the digital noise becomes apparent. With each new generation of cameras, however, the low light performance improves at an astonishing rate.

TIP:

One of the best tips that I can give you if you want to take truly creative angling photographs is that you must be prepared to sacrifice your fishing when great photo opportunities open up. This is where fishing with a good friend is so important. Being prepared to put the rod down and pick the camera up is perhaps the greatest sacrifice an angler can make and few are prepared to do it. That is why many angling magazine features and websites lack photographs with impact. The fact is that what are often the prime times for biting fish are also often the time when great images can be taken – at dawn and dusk, for example.

There are also some shots that mean virtually leaving the rod at home. Leaping fish, for example, are very difficult to get if you have a rod in your hand. Images of jumping fish can usually only be obtained by being prepared, with the camera switched on, the light metered and the aperture and shutter speed set. Since light will change many times in the day you will need to constantly check that the camera is set correctly – something you cannot do while fishing. You also need to anticipate when a fish will jump and that means being ready from the time that it is hooked.

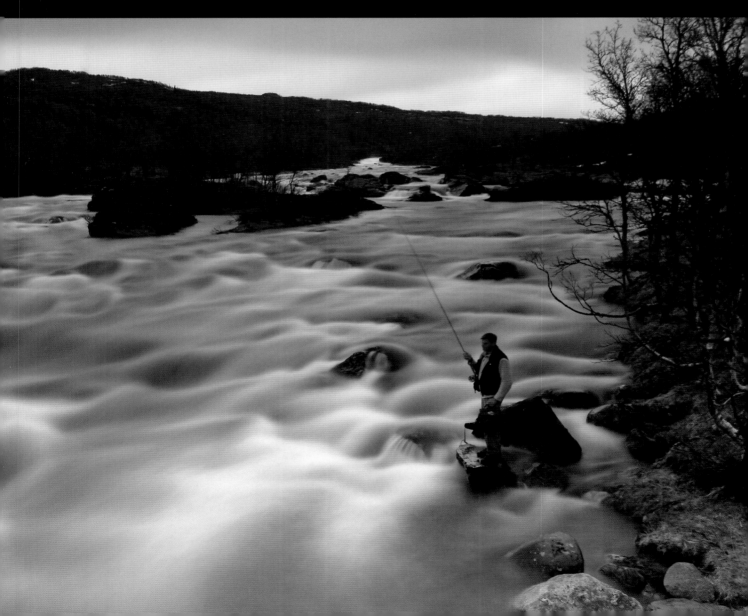

The relationship between apertures, shutter speeds and ISO's is very important. It is important not just to get correct exposures but also when deciding to hand hold or tripod mount the camera. The end result of hand holding at low shutter speeds is camera shake caused by your hands shaking, albeit minutely, while the shutter is open. To avoid camera shake, we have two options. We can either widen the aperture to deliver a higher shutter speed or increase the ISO.

ISO – How it Works

Set at ISO 50, with an aperture of f16, our camera tells us that the correct shutter speed is 1/10th of a second – too slow to hand hold the camera. The answer is to increase the ISO until we can hand hold without producing camera shake.
ISO 50 - 1/10th
ISO 100 – 1/20th
ISO 200 – 1/40th
ISO 400 – 1/80th
ISO 800 – 1/160th
ISO 1600 – 1/320th

Widening the aperture will always have a price in terms of depth of field and may or may not deliver the result that you want. Increasing the ISO setting will deliver a faster shutter speed and still produce a good exposure but at the cost of poorer saturation, contrast and increased digital noise. Many of these problems can be ironed out with software in post production but there is a limit and many photographs involve a compromise.

With all photography, choosing the right combination of Aperture, shutter speed and ISO speed is the ultimate control that dictates how the image will look. A camera on auto mode puts all of these things together and attempts to come up with a good exposure. In reality, the modes that most compact and DSLR cameras feature such as 'portrait', 'action or sports', 'landscape' etc., are simply the camera setting an aperture and working out a shutter speed to go with it.

When you choose one of these modes, the camera defaults to a set aperture

ABOVE

A sailfish greyhound leaps across the surface in Costa Rica. The wide aperture and fast shutter speed have worked their magic. The shutter speed is 1/3000th of a second at f5.6.

depending on what it thinks you want to achieve. With 'sports' for example, it will default to a high ISO and choose a wide aperture to deliver a fast shutter speed. With landscape it will default to f11 or f16 and choose a high ISO because a slower shutter speed will make it difficult to hand hold.

This is a great example of why relying on auto or other modes is ultimately not the answer. Take the landscape – you may be happy to work with a very low exposure and the lowest ISO setting to deliver the best contrast, details and colour because by using a tripod and remote release long exposures are not a problem for you.

With the action shot, let's say the camera is happy to default to f4 with a shutter speed of 1/500th of a second. This is fine for capturing a casting shot and getting the flex of the rod. Yet, when you are trying to capture an image of a leaping salmon, a shutter speed of at least 1000th is required. By putting the camera on manual, upping the ISO to 800 and reducing the

aperture to f2.8 you can get what you want a shutter speed of 1000th of a second or more and one that the sports mode would probably not have come up with.

These are situations when auto and picture modes will let you down. Av mode is certainly better. You fix the aperture and the camera gives a shutter speed. By pushing up the ISO you can increase that shutter speed until you reach the number that you want. Alternatively, you can use manual mode and exercise exact control of all of the variables. When you get to this standard you are fast on the way to becoming a good photographer.

Phew! That's the really technical stuff over and done with, I am pleased to say. Nonetheless, you must read and re-read this chapter so that you clearly understand the relationship between aperture, shutter speed and ISO setting. These are the vital building blocks of good photography and the better you understand them the easier it will be for you to capture great images.

BELOW

Dawn and dusk are the key times for evocative angling images. The light is at its best - soft and subdued. Here, Mick Brown prepares to make his first cast on the famous Throop fishery on the Dorset Stour. The sun has just risen and the skeletal forms of the winter trees are just visible through the fiery mist. A silhouette treatment works very well with this image, creating a strong composition that emphasises the eerie landscape. I have opened up just enough to retain a hint of detail in the trees and vegetation. A graduated ND filter has been used to hold back the sky and balance the light. 70mm, 1/500th second at f16, ISO 100.

Chapter Six

LIGHT AND ANGLING PHOTOGRAPHY

Ever since the days of the great landscape and portrait artists, there have been rules that dictate whether we find an image pleasing or not: the masters understood the importance of how to frame and compose a scene and also how to use light. They created a number of rules that still hold today. Yet rules are made to be broken and a really good photographer knows when to throw the rule book out of the window and when to stick to the classic method. The way that a scene or subject is captured, framed and lit has a direct effect on how it makes us feel.

Lighting is perhaps the greatest influence. Depending on how something is lit it can make us feel relaxed and comfortable or uneasy. The same scene or subject can be made to appear benign and soothing or dramatic, even moody. This holds good for all forms of photography. Sometimes we can control light or add light using special lighting, reflectors, diffusers and other devices or we can choose to shoot when light is at its most dramatic.

Since most angling photographs are taken in normal daylight conditions, I will begin with some advice about regular daylight photography. First of all, you should understand that the main daylight hours are often poor for certain forms of angling photography, notably landscape. The exception to this is when we get stormy weather, mist or other weather extremes that make the light more interesting. That is not to say we should ignore regular daylight. Indeed, taking pictures in the middle of the day is usually better suited for action, trophy or macro photography. Bright sunlight is great for action imaging because plenty of light means fast shutter speeds. Leaping fish, bending rods and explosions of water can be captured with shutter speeds of 1/500th of a second or faster and this is usually only practical in strong light. Having said this, really bright sunny days that give harsh, contrasting light are not so good for most forms of imaging, including action shots. Perfect conditions for this form of photography is bright but diffused light that gives more even tones and richer colours.

BELOW
The use of a reflector has transformed this return shot. Strong light has been bounced back onto the fish and the backdrop of pond leaves. The control of light, contrast, and subject has created a stunning image that sums up not only the beauty of the fish but also its environment. The warmth of the image creates a 'nostalgic' feel in keeping with the way most anglers feel about this super little fish.

Action Photography

The key to capturing action shots is to prepare. You should be ready, lens fitted for the action. Action shots are among the most dynamic and exciting in angling. There are two that immediately spring to mind – the casting shot, with the rod flexed and the action shot when the fish is at the net.

1.   Mount the lens that will enable you to get what you want. For a casting shot, a long lens is often good, between 200 and 300mm because its shallow depth of field isolates the caster. We want the subject to fill the frame and we are seeking to hit the shutter when the rod is at full flex

2.   A wide lens is often better for fish and angler action shots. They allow you to get closer to the action and pull in more of the scene. They are especially good if you can wade out into shallow water and shoot the fish and angler front on. They are also good when shooting 'over the shoulder.'

3.   Decide on the f-stop setting. A shallow depth of field setting around f4 or f5.6 is often perfect for both lenses because with the long lens we will get a shallow depth of field whilst with the wide lens, though technically shallow, the depth of field will be sufficient to make both angler and fish in focus. The shutter speed with the long lens is critical because we can only freeze the cast with shutter speeds of 1/500th of a second or more but it is less critical with the wider lens. Make some practice shots in the position that you intend to shoot from and set the focus on the lens to manual.

4.   Set the flash (most times some fill-flash will improve the image and help to 'freeze' any action) to 'stand-by.'

5.   Experiment with some test exposures and then set the camera to manual. Set the aperture and shutter speed in manual mode. If the light changes visibly (if the sun disappears behind clouds, for example), be prepared to repeat the process.

6.   If shooting a cast you want to get the maximum curve in the rod. To do this you will need to fire a burst of shots and to anticipate the cast. Fire the shutter just

before you think that you need to. This type of shot requires practice to get the timing right.

7.   With the wide angle shot, you can shoot more intuitively, firing off shots with camera held away from your body, high and low to create funky angles. Sometimes these can be the best shots of all.

8.   Try to keep one eye on what is happening with the fish at all times. You neither want to knock the fish-of-a-lifetime off your friend's line nor do you want to miss the moment that it clears the water or rolls on the surface.

ABOVE

Mick Brown casts for Rainbow trout in the early evening. Stormy skies threaten overhead as a shaft of sunlight breaks through the gloom and lights Mick up as if he were on a stage. These periods of intense, directional light are the catalyst for some of the best landscape and action images. This was no exception. 200mm, 1/250th sec at f4, ISO 200

Macro photography is often best in th
middle of the day too. As anglers we ge
opportunities to photograph wild plant
insects and other great macro subject
more often than most. Macro is deal
with in a separate chapter later on bu
suffice to say the best times for macro
work are not, as you might expect
bright, sunny days but rather days wher
the light is subdued or diffused by thin
cloud. When the light is 'soft' both
trophy and macros shots look their bes
because there are no harsh shadows and
contrasts to make skin or natural tones
look ugly. Rather the tones are soft with
beautifully saturated colours. We have
also dealt with basic trophy or 'catch'
photography in an earlier chapter bu
there is advice later in this chapter abou
how to take more dramatic trophy shots
by using low light and fill-flash.

Some of the nicest angling photographs
can be taken on bright sunny days wher
the sky is dotted with cotton wool clouds
it is the classic feel-good scene with azure
blue skies and plenty of light. Close-up
photography in any form requires the use
of fill-flash or a reflector (see later) to iron
out any harsh, contrast or shadows. Using
fill-flash is pretty straightforward: simply
connect a flash-gun or use the camera
built in flash and leave it on auto
Modern cameras are superb at working
out how much fill flash is needed to
knock out shadow areas.

LEFT

This shot of Ed Brown trolling on Loch Awe
illustrates the use of wide-angle lenses in boats.
Here, my objective was to gain a sense of the
towering and overpowering presence of the walls
of the Pass of Brander closing in around the
angler. I chose a low viewpoint and positioned
the sun behind Ed to eliminate lens flare. After
metering the exposure for the sky and hillside, I
had to use fill-flash to illuminate Ed and prevent
him from being reduced to silhouette. A diffuser
was fitted to the flashgun. 18mm, 1/30th sec a
f22, ISO 100, fill-flash.

Wider angle stuff, involving landscapes and fishing scenes do not involve flash, although you may use a reflector to throw some light back onto any important foreground objects. When the sun is bright and the sky blue, colours can get a little bleached out. This is the time to fit a circular polarising filter to your lens. These filters block out glare and improve highlight detail. They also have the added benefit of saturating colours.

Circular filters need to be rotated according to how you hold the camera: vertical or horizontal (or, in 'photo speak,' portrait or landscape). To get it right, point the lens either at some water or a portion of blue sky away from the sun. As you rotate the filter, you will see that the glare on the water is dramatically reduced and the colour of the sky deepens. When this is at its optimum you have found the correct position for the filter.

Remember, however, that whilst many angling shots taken in bright light will benefit from the polarising filter, the filter blocks light and you will lose shutter speed. The shutter speed for the shot when compared to photographs taken without the filter will drop by two stops. For example, the sunny 16 says that on a

BELOW

Here, I wanted to retain the spectacular colours in the stormy evening sky and to bring out the colours in the stones that had just been soaked during a rainstorm. The background has been exposed for the highlights to keep that dramatic sky, but additional work has been done to ensure that the stones in foreground and Jens are not under exposed. To light the stones, I bounced light in off a reflector and added fill-flash at a reduced amount from the auto setting (flash gun on manual). I used another off-camera flash, bounced off a second reflector, to illuminate Jens with warm light. The low viewpoint emphasises the dramatic sky. 16mm, 1/50th sec at ISO 200, two flashguns mounted off camera with reflectors.

bright day at f16, the correct shutter speed will be close to 1/125th of a second. This means that if you fit a polariser, the shutter speed will drop to 1/30th of a second and this will make hand holding with anything but wide angle lenses likely to result in lens blur. You will need to either use a tripod or, if you require faster shutter speeds to include some action or movement, take the ISO up by one or two stops. If we are shooting as ISO 100 with a shutter speed of 1/30th, at ISO 200 it will be 1/60th and at ISO 400 it will be back to 1/125th. The most commonly used f-stop or aperture for daylight landscape photography is f11 – this gives

good foreground to background focus. Big blue skies often deserve the 'big sky treatment. I like to keep the camera low, include lots of sky and try to create a towering image. Getting the sky reflected in slick, calm water is always another winner. Both shots work really well with a polariser because the contrast and colour saturation is crisp and strong.

Quality of light, its direction and strength is what often makes the difference between a mediocre photograph and a really good one – a maxim that is never more true than with landscape photographs. Most landscape scenes appear most dramatic at the extremes of the day when the light temperature changes. The change in light temperature causes a shift in the way both we see light and the way the camera records it. We are all familiar with some of the spectacular colours that can accompany dawn and sunset. This is caused by lower than normal light temperature (daylight is 6500 Kelvin). When the light temperature drops, the colour spectrum in the sky shifts and that is why we see some of the spectacular pinks, mauve, purples, reds and oranges. While our own eyes adjust quickly to the shift in colour and to some extent compensate for it a camera cannot do so, the end result being images with super saturated colours that are more vivid than the eye can detect.

Different types of light, such as artificial tungsten and other sources such as candle light etc., have different temperatures too. We do not see this as clearly as a camera records this shift in temperature. Our eyes are superb at filtering out the colour casts caused by differing light temperatures but cameras are not so adept. Images shot under different forms of artificial light take on strange colour casts. Regular light bulbs and candles, for example, give a strong 'warm' cast while tungsten light is cold and appears blue. Film cameras were equally as sensitive to these colour casts as digital cameras. In the old days, photographers fitted warming or cooling filters to the lens when shooting in artificial light. The device used in the digital camera to correct these 'casts' is the white balance facility. It is very important and has a strong bearing on lighting an image the way the eye sees it.

Changing the Way Light is Recorded with White Balance Settings

All good DSLR cameras have a white balance setting facility. Most good compacts allow you to change the white balance too. For most photography, the white balance can be set to 'auto.' This is usually the factory default setting for the camera. The camera measures the light and sets the white balance accordingly. For most images, using the correct white balance will produce the best and most natural-looking image but it is not always so. Creative photography is sometimes about breaking the rules and this principle sometimes applies to white balance settings.

Modern photo editing software makes it possible to tweak the white balance during post production and small errors made by the camera can easily be corrected. Those of us whom shoot 'raw' (as opposed to the more often used 'j-peg' format) can set any white balance we want without altering the quality of the photo.

However, deliberate white balance shifts can be made to alter the appearance of a photograph. If you shoot with camera 'raw' you can keep the white balance setting on the camera to auto and tweak it afterwards using 'Photoshop' or 'Lightroom' but if you shoot 'j-peg' (as most do) it is best to perform the shift in camera. This is quite easy: simply find the button or dial that allows you to select the white balance manually and use it override the camera's auto mechanism. This way, you can experiment with different white balance settings when shooting in normal daylight or after dark and gauge the effects.

So why would you want to do it? Shifting the white balance produces images that take on different colour casts. The light appears to be either warmer (more orange/yellow) or cooler (blue) when you shift the white balance setting. I rarely warm up images with the white balance feature (I prefer to use a warm up filter either on the lens or in post-production) but I often cool the light down. This is achieved by activating the white balance setting for 'tungsten' light.

In regular use, this feature is used to make tungsten light appear natural when taking photographs lit by it. While our eye will adjust to the change in light temperature, the camera does not do so and photos taken under tungsten light take on a blue cast. Take an image in broad daylight with the tungsten white balance activated and the shot will take on a blue cast. Though this might appear at first unnatural, the result can be a very soothing image or one that conveys a sense of cold or chill. It is particularly good when shooting early morning scenes in frost, for example, or when a flat clam lake is shrouded in mist. Colours tend to get de-saturated when taking images this way and with some simple toning techniques the images can be stunning.

I also use the tungsten setting for night photography. I find the shift to blue produces photographs that look like we think a night image should look – a little bit like the blue lighting used for night work in movies.

Another practical way to use a white balance shift is to set the balance to the 'cloudy day' or 'shaded' setting. This warms the image up slightly and is especially good when taking photographs of autumn leaves or images that have strong autumn colours in them. Whilst I much prefer to use a filter at the time of shooting to achieve this, those whom do not have warm-up or chocolate filters may find this tip useful.

Dawn and dusk can transform scenes. A shot of the lake might look OK in the middle of the day but shoot the same scene when the sky is washed with fabulous colours and the result is a spectacular shot. The same can be said of coastal photography. In the middle of a rather flat day, the sky looks washed out and the sea is an insipid grey colour. The same scene in the early morning or evening will see the sky transformed into a wash of colour and the sea-scape likewise. Bear in mind that dawn and dusk often sees a drop in wind, smoothing troubled water and we have a great recipe for photography. I love to see the surface of the river or lake like a mirror, reflecting back the hues of the heavens.

Light also changes angle at the extremes of the day. Low, directional light can bring a photograph to life. It produces beautiful, even light with a golden cast. This type of light is good for all kinds of photography – especially trophy shots.

Landscapes benefit from a low sun. Colours change, shadows lengthen and texture increases. Peaks are still bathed in sun while valleys are shaded. The landscape suddenly appears three dimensional through the viewfinder!

RIGHT

Hampton Loade on the River Severn at dawn. On a freezing cold day, this shot was taken just after first light. The river is starting to freeze up and thick frost coats the landscape. By shooting in camera raw and shifting the white balance to give the image a slightly blue tint, the sense of cold is heightened.

BELOW

This image of lone fly fisher enjoying the dawn on Lake Storsjoen, southern Norway, benefits from postproduction. A panoramic crop has been applied to exaggerate the mirror image effect of the mountains reflected in the flat calm lake. A shift in the white balance toward the tungsten setting has cooled the image down and given it a soothing blue cast. The ability of changing white balance settings without damaging the image is one of the benefits of shooting camera raw.

ABOVE

Dawn breaks and the swim is flooded with warm light. This shot benefits from the use of warm white balance setting. The quality of the light is everything in this image. Taken half an hour later when the sun would have been higher in the sky would have resulted in a less

Choosing where you fish to create the best photo opportunities is something that few anglers think about. I'm not suggesting that you forsake the hotspot or honey hole for a cesspit swim that holds no fish but provided that there is no need to be in an exact spot to catch fish, it makes sense to choose an area to fish that offers good photo possibilities.

Usually this is where the light will be best at the times of day that you will fish. At dawn, for example, you might want to face east to catch the rising sun while at dusk shooting toward the West is going to be favourite.

Points and promontories are particularly good because they allow you to change camera angles and work with the light. On the coast, the choice is even more stark – you will want to be on the side of the land facing West in the afternoon and on the East-facing side in the morning.

You should also look for fishing areas that allow you the best photo opportunities according to the type of images that you are trying to capture. The choice at its simplest level can mean not fishing against a backdrop that does not lend itself well to action or trophy photography while at a more creative level, when taking landscape dominated scenes for example, more planning is required.

Calm lakes always look more soothing for landscapes than those affected by wind; rivers that wind and bend are much more photogenic than straight stretches; venues with flat land and open trees are great for sunsets and silhouettes; mountains and hills make for fantastic textured landscapes. Even urban venues complete with industrial buildings and graffiti can be interesting when shot in a 'gritty' way using black and white or photo toning/bleaching post production.

The major problem with landscape photography at the extremes of the day is that there is often a huge imbalance between the amounts of light being reflected back of the components of the scene. The sky and water will be bright and filled with brilliant colour while the foliage tends to be dark and lacking brilliance. There are several solutions to this problem.

The first is to turn the camera around and shoot away from the sun, where the light falls on the landscape. It will be beautifully lit by warm light. Most of the time, however, the best results will be obtained by shooting angling scenes into the sun. There are, however, some problems with this, the first being that you should avoid looking directly at the sun through the viewfinder and the second being the problem of lens flare. Lens flare is a halo of light, often in overlapping

ABOVE

I love skies. Whenever I can, I like to make interesting skies a key theme of the images I take and fiery sunsets like this one cry out to dominate the composition. At dusk, the trout reservoir is almost blood red , reflecting the spectacular hues of a sunset lighting the retreating storm clouds. Getting images like this is tricky. I used fill flash, with the flash gun mounted off the camera on a bracket and fitted with a diffuser. I tried several exposures on manual flash output to get just the right amount of illumination for the angler. The sky is slightly under-exposed to retain the drama, colour and detail.

RIGHT

Guide Anders Forsberg shares a boat with Ed Brown and the duo fish for pike. Gorgeous evening light floods the scene and catches the edge of

1.   Lens flare will be dramatically reduced if you deploy a lens hood.

2.   Angling the camera even slightly away from head on to the sun will further eliminate flare.

3.   Clean optics are a must for reducing flare – always carry some lens tissue and some liquid lens cleaner to thoroughly clean both the lens element and any filters used.

4.   Using a high f-number (usually favoured when shooting landscape) will burn the sun down to more of a pin-prick than the bright blob of fiery orange that shooting with a wide aperture will produce.

5.   Waiting until the sun is half hidden by the edge of a cloud will eliminate flare.

6.   To avoid damage to your eyes, mount the camera on a tripod, fire test shots and shift the frame, zoom or in camera settings without looking directly into the sun.

Shooting sunrise and sunset landscapes can produce truly memorable images but unless you are shooting silhouette, when taking landscapes, for example, a filter will need to be used. This is to even out the different amounts of light being given off by the bright sky and the darker landscape. A filter can be avoided if you take a range of exposures and merge them to create an HDR image (see later) and this technique is becoming more common.

For a single image, the difference in the light values on the different portions of the image will mean that the camera can either get the sky correctly exposed (in which case the landscape will appear under-exposed) or the landscape exposed correctly (in which case the sky will be washed out and over exposed) but it cannot do both. However by using a neutral density graduated filter you can expose for the landscape and hold back some of the light from the sky, creating a balanced image, as the eye sees it, with detail and colour retained in the sky. I have already mentioned these neutral density graduated filters but to recap, they are rectangular filters made of glass or polymer with a coating of neutral grey. The grey gets darker toward the top of the filter and the filter is clear in the lower half. Fit the filter into its holder and position the start of the grey section where the landscape meets the sky. You can tweak the filter up and down to get a natural, well-balanced image. The strength of the grad filters available varies from 0.3 (1 stop) to 1.2 (4 stops). I always carry a full set and experiment until I find the effect I like.

Even in the middle of the day light can be spectacular. I have taken some memorable shots in thick mist, for example. The right moment is when the sun breaks through the mist giving the scene and ethereal quality. Shoot the angler in silhouette in these conditions and position them against the backdrop of mist and breaking sun. The result is that the mist looks on fire – a perfect recipe for some evocative angling images. Exposures are pretty simple in this situation. Simply put your camera's meter on 'spot' and point it at the sun. The exposure will be for the brightest part of the image, rendering everything else to silhouette. This includes the trees (they take on a skeletal appearance especially in winter).

How to Shoot Silhouette

Silhouettes are among the simplest images to obtain because exposure is straightforward, allowing you to concentrate on composition. Silhouette images should be simple and feature strong lines, contrasting the subject against a high contrast background – usually a colourful sky.

1. The best time to shoot silhouettes is in the evening. The sun will be low and golden. Clear days are very good for this.

2. Choose a strongly defined subject and make sure that you position the camera so that the subject pokes over the horizon. A common mistake with anglers is that the camera is not positioned low enough to see that they are actually fishing. Try to make sure that hands and fishing rod break the horizon.

3. You can also silhouette anglers against brightly lit water by adopting a high viewpoint.

4. Try to position the subject where it will have a strong impact. The rule of thirds (see later) is a good way judging this and central compositions can be strong too. Needless to say, the subject will need to be positioned against the brightest part of the sky. Getting the sun directly behind the model is a great way of getting a strong silhouette and avoiding lends flare (these are annoying concentric circles of light caused by the light refracting through the lens elements. (Scratches and less than spotlessly clean optics make them much worse). When the sun is really low and about to disappear behind the horizon, you can shoot directly into it without flare. Note, however, that looking at the sun directly through the viewfinder is never advisable - it can cause damage to your eyes. A tripod mounted camera with a cable release will help with this or you could use the 'Live View' feature.

5. Set the camera to a wide aperture. f4 or f5.6 is perfect. You are not going to capture landscape detail so it is pointless using a narrow aperture. The benefit of the wide aperture is that you should get a fast shutter speed. Switch the ISO to 100

6. Meter against the brightest part of the sky with the camera's built-in meter set to 'spot.' Alternatively, take a test shot with the camera on 'auto.' If the exposure is too bright, you can either switch to manual and up the shutter speed until you get what you want or use the exposure compensation facility in AV mode. Compact cameras too can take good silhouette shots if they can be switched over to one of these modes.

7. Take the shot and check that the contrast is good and that what you have photographed in silhouette looks strong. With anglers, ensure that you can see that they are fishing. If not, try taking a lower angle shot or shift position until you can clearly see what the model is doing.

8. Sunset is a great time to shoot silhouettes of rods flexing. Low apertures at f2.8 or f4 with the exposure set to the brightest part of the sky will produce silhouettes that show the rod fully flexed. The shutter speeds will be high (between 1/500th and 1/2000th is perfect).

RIGHT
The Throop fishery on the Dorset Stour is once again the scene of a fantastic sunrise. A classic silhouette shot with the rule of thirds once again evident.

BELOW
After a whole week of fishing on the Rio Grande, Argentina, I had yet to see one of its famous sunsets. On the last evening, we were blessed with a cracker. Here, an angler makes his last cast of the week under the watchful eye of guide, Diego. This is a classic silhouette shot. 16mm, 1/200th sec at f5.6, ISO 320.

I have also taken some interesting shots when the landscape is still shrouded with mist and there is no sign of the sun. This situation is perfect for some 'minimalist' stuff where you take a simple subject, an angler on the bank or a fisherman in a boat, perhaps and deliberately exclude any familiar objects. These shots, with the angler shrouded in mist have a stark, almost eerie feel to them and I never tire of taking them. Sadly, in our wet, windy country, the opportunities are rather scarce. Metering can be tricky too and you will certainly need to over-expose from the camera's meter reading to keep the mist pale. Though not as confusing to the camera's meter as snow (see previous chapter), mist can fool the meter by as much as 1.5 f-stops. The trick is to spot meter against the mist and then try 'opening-up' by a stop or even one and a half stops.

ABOVE

This image of a lone angler in a float tube, fishing a wilderness lake in Norway illustrates the power of including anglers in landscape images. The angler is placed in the top right portion of the grid and adds a focal point to the image.

The sense of space is deliberate and emphasises the loneliness of wilderness fishing. The lower vegetation is deliberately blurred to create a natural frame. The shot is made by the beautiful pastel colours in the sky and their contrast with the pale, cool foreground.

RIGHT

Pike angler, Kev Shaw, emerges from the mist while fishing on a very cold morning on Lough Ramor, Ireland. With this image, I have deliberately included lots of empty space to emphasise the lonely feeling that anyone fishing in fog will have experienced. The photograph has an eerie, haunted feel and the isolation of the big water angler is obvious. The placement of angler and boat on the lines of intersection of the bottom right third of the image is classic - the image looks pleasing to the eye and the boat has space to 'travel into.' 200mm lens, 1/500th sec, f4, iso 800.

Opening Up – Stopping Down

What do we mean by 'opening up' or 'stopping down'? The answer is that if we open up, we either lower the shutter speed or drop the f-number down to allow more light in. Conversely, if we stop down it means that we notch up the shutter speed or increase the f-number to reduce the light. In both cases it is most usual to change the shutter speed, not the aperture.

If we 'open up' from 1/125th of a second the recipe is as follows:

1/3 stop: 1/100th (this being approx 1/3 of the difference between the next full f-stop at 1/60th of a second)
1 stop: 1/60th
2 Stops: 1/30th

If we 'stop down' from 1/125th, it goes as follows.

1/3 stop: 1/160th(this being approx 1/3 of the difference to the next full stop added on
1 stop: 1/250th
2 stops: 1/500th

So why do we 'open-up' or 'stop down'? This is most usually to overcome the problems caused by tricky light conditions fooling the camera's meter. Excessively bright objects or subjects can dominate the light reflecting back from a scene, distorting the meter reading. Classic examples being bright or very dark water, a very bright sky, snow, mist etc,

Even in the middle of the day light can become very spectacular – when the sun bursts from behind the clouds after heavy rain, for example. I love this type of light because it always looks so dramatic. The big clouds are backlit and heavily contrasted. All kinds of angling images look really good when the sun bursts through. The light is invariably spectacular and strong. It creates shafts of light that act like huge spot lamps on parts of the landscape. Boat shots on waterscapes always look good in this type of stormy weather – they convey a sense of drama – but so too do 'bivvies' and tents. Shooting such scenes that

show the angler or his boat, tent etc. being dwarfed by the landscape helps to convey a sense of the power of nature.

Use this strong directional light, when the skies are dark but the sun is bright should not be confined to landscape Action shots, for example, where the angler is casting against a big, heavy sky or playing a fish look fantastic. The bright light illuminates the subject and creates a strong contrast against the dark backdrop of the clouds. Try to include plenty of sky in these photographs – this will help to build the drama of the shot

Catch shots, too, look great in these conditions. It is a little bit like shooting in an outdoor studio. Position the subject in the light and shoot against either a strongly lit backdrop (golden light on reed beds or bank side vegetation looks great) or simply position the subject and the fish against a dark section of sky. By adopting a low viewpoint (lying down and angling the camera up toward the subject so that a lot of sky is included) will create a truly moody trophy shot.

LEFT

Quality of light is everything in photography and this shot of my wife, Anne Marit, by a campfire in the mountains of Norway, proves it. Heavy storm clouds break momentarily to release a shaft of intense early evening light, creating beautiful contrast. An hour earlier, or possibly later and this image would have been nowhere near as powerful. Indeed, breaks in the cloud when stormy skies are present often present photographers with 'golden' moments that last for no more than a few seconds. 32mm, 1/30th sec f6.7 ISO 100

Advanced Technique · Creating Moody Trophy Shots Using Creative Flash

If you read your flashgun manual you will realise that most decent flashes are very sophisticated and are capable of delivering almost total control over their light output. A good camera and flashgun delivers amazing performance. The camera reads the amount of light coming from the scene and works out how much flash needs to be outputted to achieve a well-lit image. It even takes account of the focal length of the lens and the distance from the subject to the lens.

This is all performed on the auto settings and even when the auto setting on the camera is turned off, the flash, when set to auto will work out the correct amount of light to accompany the exposure you have set. The problems and opportunities come when the flashgun is taken off auto and set to manual. Many photographers are afraid to do this. However, being brave enough to use the flash on manual is the key to those creative low light portrait shots. In other words, to create really great low light portraits you should read the flashgun manual and learn how to use the manual settings.

Moody trophy shots against heavy skies can be taken even when strong light is not falling on the subject. One of my favourite techniques on dull days is to set the camera at a low angle looking up at the subject. I like to include plenty of sky in these shots so open landscapes are perfect. Make sure that there is plenty of 'texture' in the sky. It can look angry – in fact the blacker it is and the more defined the texture of the clouds, the more I like it.

The image is deliberately under exposed to keep that important sky detail and filled in with flash used to create a good exposure of the angler. The effect is that the sky is dark, moody and full of texture while the subject is well-lit. Control of the flash is essential for this type of shot and I often use two flash guns that 'communicate' with each other and fire at the same time (most top quality flash guns can be 'synchronised' in this way.

I usually favour a camera mounted flash and a further flash gun positioned to the side of the subject and angled with the head up. Most often, the flash guns will need to be set to manual and programmed to fire above the auto setting to create the correct exposure. In effect, we are under-exposing

the background but using the correct flash output for the foreground.

To achieve this, the flash guns are set to 'manual' and the flash output is tweaked up by anything between a half and three full stops. I have also used a similar technique in twilight, when the sun has set but the sky retains some colour, by tweaking the flashgun on its manual setting. Many of you will have experienced the frustrating effect of flash photography after sunset. What happens is that the auto settings on the camera usually cause it to default to 1/60th of a second.

This is way too fast to retain any colour or detail in the sky but the subject is OK because they are lit with flash. The result is a dusk picture that looks as if it is fully dark because the background is underexposed to black. This is a pity because twilight shots with some colour retained in the sky always look better than those with a black background.

What the auto settings do not take account of, however, is that with a tripod it is possible to use low exposures and still get sharp images. Even at shutter speeds as low as 1/10th of a second, a burst of flash will

LEFT

The predatory ferox trout of Lake Mjosa in Norway are legendary. This trophy shot shows a magnificent, fully-spotted fish being returned. I wanted to include the twilight colours in the sky and the composition and exposure were carefully considered. To minimise distress to the fish, Mick and I had rehearsed the shot and this exposure took very little time. Mick is positioned to occupy just over half of the frame with the fish filling the empty space below the right-hand side of the boat. The twilight sky occupies the upper right portion and the angle of the boat pulls the eye through the image. Fill-flash was used at a reduced level to avoid blowing out the sky to black (this would have happened with the camera and flashgun set to auto). I opted for a manually set, long exposure to retain the colour in the sky with the flash tweaked down and bounced off the white portion of the boat. With short, wide-angle lenses, it is possible to handhold shots with long exposures and use the flash to freeze any slight movement. 28mm, 1/10th of a second at f6.7, ISO 200.

LEFT

*In this shot, rather than use an auto exposure, the
ISO setting was pushed to 200 and combined with
a manual exposure to 'grab' some of the ambient
light in the twilight sky. Two flashguns set at a
lower power than 'auto' provides enough light to
produce a perfect exposure of captor without
overwhelming the natural light in the background.
Using the camera on auto would have reduced the
background to black. This image illustrates the
benefit of learning to take the camera off auto and
use manual settings.*

The next stage is to set the flash. Turn the
gun on and set it to manual. Take several
shots at 1/16th, 1/8th, ¼ and ½ of a stop
under. One of these outputs should produce
a decent result with a nicely lit subject and a
colourful twilight sky. Bearing in mind the
welfare of the fish, you must familiarise
yourself with how to meter through the
camera, set the camera to fully manual and
adjust both shutter speed and aperture and
to do be able to set the flash output to
manual. This should be done in advance of
a fishing trip and rehearsed. If you cannot
make these adjustments quickly, do not
attempt it. The safest way is to rehearse the
procedure without a fish in the image.

Most conventional portrait shots look best
on dull days when the light is soft and
subdued. Harsh shadows and high contrast
ruin trophy photographs and the softer
shadows and contrasts of diffused light are
much better. This is also true of wildlife and
macro photography. Subdued, diffused light
caused by the sun being filtered through thin
cloud creates superbly saturated colours and
allows the photographer to capture a huge
range of tones and detail.

Bright sunlight can look good provided that
fill flash or reflected light is used and
provided that the sky is blue and dramatic.
Controlling contrast is the key here and that
is where the reflectors and flash guns come
in – they fill in the harsh shadows caused by
bright light. The increased contrast on
bright, sunny days often 'bleaches out'
colours but this can be overcome to some
extent by the use of polarising filters and lens
hoods. Wide angle, big sky photographs are
probably best suited to bright sunny days.

freeze the subject and everything will
appear sharp. Seasoned pros know this and
can even shoot hand held at low shutter
speeds with a burst of flash and get sharp
pictures. The trick is to get just the right
amount of flash so that the background is
not overpowered and nor is the subject.
Get it right and the result is a stunning
image where fish and captor are well lit and
the sky retains a deep, rich colour.

This is a tricky technique but one that
never fails to produce impressive results.
It works best with a wide angle lens, set to
its minimum focal length (somewhere

between 14 and 20mm), so that you can
be close to the subject. Bearing in mind
the welfare of the fish, you will need to
work quickly. The best way is to use the
camera's meter to establish quickly the
background exposure. Set the aperture
(usually f5.6) and push up the ISO speed
until you get a shutter speed of between
10th and 1/30th of a second at f5.6. Take
a test shot. Is the sky too dark or too light.
Now switch to manual and set the
aperture at F5.6. Using your last exposure
as a reference, tweak the shutter speed
until you take a picture that retains colour
in the sky.

With landscape photography, the biggest problem is that when light is at its most dramatic, there will often be parts of the scene that are too bright or too dark. Expose for the sky, for example, and the landscape becomes very dark and lacking in detail. Expose for the landscape and the sky becomes washed out. This is where neutral density graduated filters come in. These are fitted into a special holder and work by holding back the light in certain portions of the scene. The filters are rectangular or square and are coated with a neutral grey that holds back light but does not alter colours. The grey is applied from light to strong in a graduated effect and there are soft and hard ND Grads. Position them so that where the grey grad begins on the filter is in line with where the landscape meets the sky. The effect is that some of the light in the sky is held back, bringing the tone of the sky closer to that of the land. This balances the

amount of light and allows the photographer to expose for the darker parts of the scene and yet still keep detail in the highlights (sky). ND Graduated filters come in 0.3, 0.6. 0.9 and 1.2 (1,2,3 and 4 stops). You should use a filter that retains sky detail when you expose for the land but does not darken it excessively.

With portrait photography, subdued light is the best and it should be combined with some fill flash to fill in the shadows. A diffuser on the head of your flash gun will soften the light and make it fall more evenly, leading to more natural-looking portraits. Alternatively, try using a disc reflector. These are collapsible discs that come with a choice of reflective surfaces from black to white and silver to gold. They can be used to bounce back light by positioning the subject either with the light or to one side. They are superb for producing really beautifully lit and fully

BELOW
A pike boat is anchored on Lake Windermere and the lake, a perfect mirror, reflects soft pastel colours. The light is perfect for mid-afternoon photography - soft, and diffused - colours that would burn out in harsh light come to life. This is an idyllic angling scene and one that demonstrates just how powerful the right weather conditions can be when it comes to creating great images. 70mm, 1/125th sec, F5.6, ISO 100, ND Grad, two stops, to hold back the sky.

in portraits with no harsh shadow areas. I tend to use white most of the time but with golden coloured or brassy fish I like a gold reflector and with silver fish I like silver. The reflector can be angled to reflect light back onto a part of the subject or all of it. It can be propped up or held by a third party. Either way, reflectors are a cheap way to create really nice photographs and they are so light and compact that they are easy to carry with your standard camera kit.

It is also possible with a disc reflector to shoot with the sun behind the subject and bounce light back onto them to fill in the shadows. This creates a halo of light behind the subject or 'rim lighting.' Done correctly, this effect looks simply stunning and is one way of creating trophy shots that really stand out from the crowd. Rim lit shots tend to work best at the extremes of the day when the sun is low in the sky.
One of my favourite photographs was shot

with a disc reflector. I wanted to capture the spray that sometimes flies off a reel when it is spinning and backlit by the sun. I tried various ways to get the 'Catherine' wheel effect before finally cracking it by simply bouncing light back onto the subject using a large reflector. The water droplets are backlit by a low sun and front lit using the reflector. The results were better than anything I had tried with twin flashguns and dark studio backdrops!

We'll finish with one of the classic angling photography techniques – dreamy water. This is the effect created whereby water looks creamy and smooth. We have all drooled over images of fly anglers standing in rivers where the water swirls like liquid ice around them. The effect is created by shooting scenes with a very low shutter speed. How is this achieved in what is clearly quite strong light? Moreover, how do pro photographers make the angler standing in the scene appear in focus and not blurred.

The answer to the well-focused angler is the easiest to deal with. This where having a good fishing friend whom can pose and stay perfectly still for a few seconds pays dividends. I have one friend in particular, Ed Brown, whom I love to use for this sort of shot. For a start, Ed is a statuesque good-looking sort of chap whom always wears the right kit. He looks like a fly fisherman should look. He is also extremely patient with me and has perfected holding poses for several seconds to order. This, and the occasional burst of fill-flash with the camera mounted away from the camera and pointed at the subject does the job.

The slowing down of the water is straightforward too. To make water 'dreamy' we need to use a shutter speed of ¼ of a second at the fastest. One full second or even two or three seconds can be necessary at certain times but be careful not to overdo the effect. In the middle of the day you can only achieve these slow shutter speeds by fitting a filter to your lens to block out the light. A polariser is a good choice because it will block to full stops. Set the camera to its lowest ISO setting (either 100 or 'L' if your camera has it), the aperture at f16 and see what the meter tells you. If the shutter speed is approaching a second in length you are in business. The

other way to achieve the slow shutter speed is to use a full ND Filter. These are neutral grey filters that do not alter colours but simply hold back light. A 1.2 ND will hold back 4 stops!

Taking the Dreamy Water Shot

1. Set the camera on a tripod and set th frame. Get your subject (if there is an angler in the scene) to stand in so that you can check the composition.

2. Set the camera's ISO setting to it lowest (either 100 or 'L').

3. Fit a filter to the lens – either a ND Filter or a polariser.

4. Put the camera on manual or AV and set the aperture at f11 or f16. If the camera's meter tells you that the correct shutter speed is ¼ of a second or less you are in business.

5. Fit a remote or cable release.

6. Ask your subject to step in to the frame.

7. Focus manually.

8. Ask the subject to hold still.

9. Take shot and repeat until you are happy

These shots are not as tricky to achieve as they first appear once you know how. Va Atkinson eat your heart out! The technique works well with all moving water be it stream, river or wave lashed sea or lake shore. It is one of the nicest angling shots to 'pull off' but if there is a downside it is becoming rather common in fly fishing magazines and websites.

This has been a necessarily long chapter because using and working with light will have the greatest impact on your angling photography. The way light falls on a subject or scene will make or break the image and can make the difference between a mediocre shot and a classic. The key is to experiment and learn to accept the failures. Eventually you will intuitively know what shots are likely to work best in differing light conditions

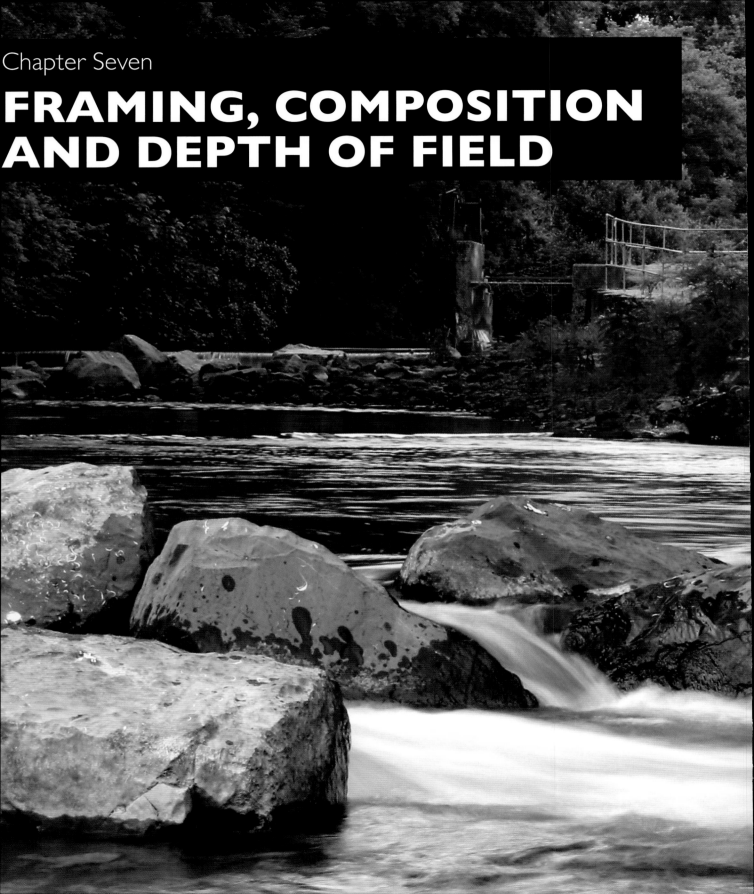

Chapter Seven

FRAMING, COMPOSITION AND DEPTH OF FIELD

In just the same way that light can change the way an image looks and feels, the same can be said of the next three building blocks. The same scene will rarely be interpreted the same way by individual photographers: that is what makes photography so fascinating because it is the way we choose to portray a scene that is our individual signature and it is this ability that gives an image 'soul.'

We record and interpret how we feel about a scene or what we see as important by the framing, the camera angle, the composition and how much of the scene we have in and out of focus. With frames and camera angles we have the ultimate power to decide what we include and what we exclude. What we exclude is just as important as what we include, perhaps more so. In some images, 'less is more.'

When we go fishing we tend to mentally filter out the distractions that we find displeasing: we ignore the ugly building or rusty car by the water's edge; we simply don't see the brightly coloured lifebelt or sign that spoils the image and so on. Many landscapes and waterscapes are ruined by certain objects, structures etc., but that does not mean that we cannot enjoy being in the place.

We look for the beauty in places and that is what we must do with the camera, framing out the distracting or ugly stuff. In addition to framing we can use shallow or deep depth of field to render parts of or the whole scene in focus. Using depth of field creatively helps us to pick out beautiful pictures from backgrounds that might at first appear chaotic or confusing. In reality we are mimicking what we do in life when we look for beauty in an imperfect environment.

Composition is often about finding order among chaos while occasionally it might be about portraying chaos. In essence it is about creating an image that portrays how we feel about a place and helping the viewer to not only to see what we see but also to see it in the same way. When things are ordered in a certain way we find the composition pleasing. This is an intuitive process and something that we don't think about in day to day life. Most good landscape photographs will have objects of interest in the foreground and will lead the eye through the frame to objects on interest in the background. They take the eye on a journey through the image to the main point of the picture. A classic example of this is a river winding down from the mountain. Our eye settles on the river and follows it until it settles on the mountain. When we look at a good landscape image our eye goes on a journey of discovery.

RIGHT

Adopting a low viewpoint and a relatively wide-angle lens creates drama. Here, Lawrie Hickman casts a salmon fly on the Dee and the low viewpoint coupled with the dark, threatening skies, makes the image dramatic. 16mm, 1/200th sec, high speed flash, ISO400.

BELOW

A very simple image of a Cuban mangrove saltwater flat at first light. No angler is needed here - the scene is serene and beautiful. The sky is filled with pastel colours that reflect on the calm surface. The mangrove plants have been reduced to silhouette to keep the emphasis on the sky and its reflection. The key focal point is the cloud with the sun rising behind it while the two mangrove bushes provide balance on the edges of the image. This shot was taken with a Hasselblad X-Pan, a panoramic film camera. The film is Fuji Velvis. 45mm lens, 1/15th sec at f11, ISO 50.

ABOVE

In this, the second of the images taken of Lawrie Hickan, spey casting on the Dee, a higher viewpoint has been adopted. This image appears more connectional and while the dark skies still threaten, the image has a more conventional and less dramatic feel. 16mm, 1/800th sec. f5.6.

Of course, we cannot move heavy or fixed objects to make a scene just the way we want to see it, our tool is to position the camera in the best place to see the scene how we want it portrayed and to use a lens that will frame out any unwanted clutter. We can also use depth of field to bring selected parts or everything in the image into sharp focus so that the details that we want the viewer to see stand out. Sometimes we can use a shallow depth of field to render the objects or parts of the scene that we regard as being less important to a vague, impressionistic blur.

The positioning of the camera is vital in achieving good composition. Take the example of the river winding down from the mountain: if we position the camera facing away from the mountain or with the river not flowing toward the camera but across the scene, it would not have the same impact as the classic image of the river winding down from the mountain into the lens. Most of us in this scenario would intuitively place the camera so that the mountain is in the background and the river flows toward us in the foreground – this is because we are all drawn to certain compositions. While other landscape scenes and images are less easy to compose, you should always pay attention to your intuition – it will often give you a good starting point.

RIGHT
This shot needs no angler to make it complete. Instead, the raw beauty of the Norwegian nature is allowed to speak for itself. It is autumn; the mountains have a fresh sprinkling of snow and the trees have turned to rich, russet hues of orange, red, and gold. The river runs clear and cold, fed by a nearby glacier and winds into the distance… Classic rule of thirds and composition. 28-70mm lens set at 44mm, 1/60th sec at f11, ISO 100.

LEFT

The Glomma, Norway's longest river, is just beginning to thaw after the long cold winter. Once again, the rule of thirds, with one third land, one third river and mountains, and one third sky, makes this a balanced composition. The key points to notice are the winding river and railroad track - these lead the eye through the picture to the distant snow-capped mountains. 34mm, 1/30th sec at f11, ISO 100.

BELOW

Jon Olav Oldren casts a beautiful line on the Verdal river in Norway. The beautiful sky helps to make this shot, as does the low angle. Note the positioning of the angler in the bottom right third, and the general use of the rule of thirds in the composition. A fast shutter speed of 1/2000th of a second freezes the action.

ABOVE

Classic composition with the winding river used to lead the eye toward the main subject. A long lens compresses the distance. There is good use of the rule of thirds here. The shot is also a classic example of what can be achieved by preparing the shot. I set the camera on a tripod, framed it, and adjusted the exposure. All my friend had to do was press the shutter!

The Rule of Thirds

The rule of thirds has long been a benchmark not just in landscape photography but in other forms of art too – especially landscape painting.

The rule of thirds says that objects or components of an image are most pleasing to the eye when they are located at key points in the frame. These key points are created by drawing three imaginary equally spaced horizontal lines on the frame and three imaginary vertical lines to create a grid. The points at which these lines intercept are the most pleasing places to put objects of interest. In other words, the objects or key parts of the scene should be arranged off centre. But some compositions also work well when the object is placed in the centre of the frame. With some images it can pay to break the rule. Nonetheless, the rule of thirds is very important when it comes to wider views and landscape but it can also be good with close-up work too.

With landscape particularly, the classic way is to have one third sky, one third land and one third foreground interest (a large rock, boat or fisherman, for example). With the object of major foreground interest placed on one of the rule of thirds interception points and the ultimate subject for the eye to be lead to on the horizon positioned on another of the rule of thirds intersection points, you have the recipe for a classic landscape image.

Strong lines and clean edges are also very useful in photography. This is why silhouettes are so pleasing to the eye. Fence lines, river banks, curving lake shores – all of these have the potential to create great photographs. Lines or shapes that lead the eye through the image from foreground to background are called 'lead-in' lines.

A classic example is a boat jetty or pier. Like a railroad track, it gradually narrows and tapers off into the distance (or at least it appears to) taking your attention with it and leading it elsewhere. Place an angler with a fishing rod at the end of the jetty and you have a winning formula for a great angling image. Generally speaking the best place to put the will either be one third up or two thirds up the image. The angler may be placed to one side if the pier curves away (at one of the intersection points) but if it is straight a central position will look better.

Creating a focal point for the eye to settle on as it follows the lead-in lines is important. A scene of a boat jetty leading our eye toward a lake is powerful but it may be more powerful if there is an angler standing at the end of the jetty or a boat with a fisherman in it on the horizon. Whatever our lead in lines take the eye to it must not be disappointing. In the case of the lake, if its a flat calm mirror reflecting back the heavens this may be enough.

With most landscape compositions key focal points should not compete. It is good to have more than one point of interest in the frame but they should not be placed in a position to compete with each other

either in terms of scale or placement. If our typical landscape image where the river winds its way down from the mountain we might place an interesting rock or fence post in the foreground to add some interest. The viewer sees the rock, follows the river and ends up looking at the mountain. This type of composition is classic but it does not work so well if the mountain and the rock are of the same size. The mountain can be smaller or bigger than the rock but if it is the same size the two points of interest are fighting with each other for the viewer's attention and the whole process of leading the eye through the image breaks down. Using different lenses will alter the sense of scale and balance the picture. A wide angle lens will make the rock large and the mountain smaller. Using a long lens, we can use part of the rock in the foreground to create a frame for the large mountain behind it (remember that telephoto lenses compress distance).

In the same way, placing two boats or two anglers at exactly the same level on the horizon will cause them to compete with each other and the viewer will not know where to settle their attention. Two boats or two anglers placed at varying distances from the camera works, however.

Sometimes a line of subjects can work really well. Imagine a row of anglers fishing off a pier. Shooting along the line of anglers and using them like a perspective or lead in line is very powerful. Shooting the same group, flat to the camera and silhouetted against the sky is strong too. Whilst the rules I have described can be broken (and sometimes should) they will at least help you to understand why an image, though well-exposed and sharp simply does not work. More often than not the culprit is composition, framing or depth of field.

A group of fishing rods propped up against a rod stand is another powerful subject. Shooting down the line so that some of the rods and reels are in focus while others are out is a good formula for an image. The same can be said of a line of flies in a fly box. By using depth of field to control how many of the items arranged in the image are in focus, how many are seen but not sharp and how many are reduced to a

BELOW

This shot of Ed Brown using a drifter float while pike fishing shows how to use composition to show an item of fishing tackle within context. The eye naturally moves from the float to the angler.

vague, impressionistic blur we can alter the way the final image looks quite dramatically. It might be for example that we want to convey a sense of the scene being 'busy.' To do this we will use a narrow aperture (high f-number) and try to retain focus on as many items in the image as possible. The 'mishmash' of so many rods being abandoned by their owners sets off chains of thought. 'Are they in the bar right now?' 'At breakfast, maybe?' It also conveys a sense that the place that the rods have been left must be a busy and popular fishing lodge.

A nice exercise for you to try is to photograph a fly box. Shoot it from different angles. Use differing depths of field. You might shoot at an angle using a medium aperture so that the flies become increasingly more blurred the further they are from the front. If you want to draw attention to one particular fly, to suggest that this is the fly to choose, for example, you could use a wide aperture, say f2.8 or f4 and reduce all the other flies in front of and behind the subject to a an

impressionistic blur. You might shoot the whole box or part of it. You might even want to zoom out to show it in its environment – sitting on a table, in hand, being inspected by the water while the owner chooses a fly.

The fly box example is a great way to prove to yourself how experimenting with camera angles, frames and depth of field can totally change the way a viewer will fell about a subject. If we photograph the box from above, flat on to the lens, all of the flies and the box will be sharp. Though useful, perhaps for showing a selection of flies with accompanying descriptions in a book or magazine, the image, though well-ordered and well-composed, is rather flat and uninteresting. If we lower the camera angle and shoot into the box from different directions, using varying depths of field to bring some or all of the flies into focus we totally change the dynamic of the subject. Viewed from different angles and using varying depths of field we can make cluttered images, isolate key flies and create depth and perspective.

ABOVE
Northern Norway is a riot of warm colour in th
autumn. This shot gives a perfect illustration
how the eye can be led through an image by usin
natural curves or bends. 28mm, 1/30th sec
f11, ISO 200, polarising filter fitted

The example with the fly box illustrates that giving thought to composition should not be limited to landscape shots. It affects macro, trophy and other forms of angling photography too. Sometimes, when you are photographing a friend with a fish, it just does not look right. Sometimes they are holding the fish awkwardly but it might also be your fault. Your camera angle is too high or too low. Generally a lower viewpoint works best and it also helps if the angler is not totally 'square on' to the lens but rather has his/her body and the fish angled but favouring the lens.

Cut off points are also very important. If you cut the shot off too close to the anglers head it might be better than cropping off the top of the head but it still looks uncomfortable. The same applies if you cut the image off too close to the fish's head, tail or belly. It just does not look balanced. Remember the rule of thirds? It comes into play again. The frame should be divided into thirds and the scene arranged accordingly. There should be one third lower frame which may be the angler's legs, the fish and hands in the middle and the angler's head at the top. A vertical (portrait) crop always looks best for these 'full body' shots. With closer crops allow some space above the head and below the fish (thirds again!)

Another classic example of the rule of thirds is when taking an action shot of an angler casting. They may be in a boat or on The bank. Invariably the best place to position the angler in the frame is one third up the frame. You might consider placing the subject two-thirds up the frame if you have another item of foreground interest such as a rock or another boat. In this case, both foreground and background focal points should be positioned on one of the intersection points of the rule of thirds, usually on opposite sides of the image. Try this and you will see.

An action shot of an angler casting in the centre of the frame rarely looks right. One third up is usually best. With sunsets, two thirds up can look good provided that the foreground has shape.

shot, which the angler is just one of the points of interest in the frame, the angler and the other focal points of interest are usually best arranged according to the 'thirds' rule. Try taking a shot of a boat with open water in the foreground and the boat in the centre of the image and you will see what I mean.

By understanding that composition can make or break an image you will learn that the camera angle and the focal length of the lens play a key role in creating order from chaos. Shifting angles or changing to a longer or wider angle lens will radically alter the composition of the scene and where the key points are arranged.

When an angler is just one component of the image (but usually the key focal point), a wide angle or medium focal length is best because this allows you to 'pull in' the environment. When the angler is intended to be just about the only focal point, a longer lens that compresses distance will frame out any other distracting elements. Telephoto lenses are superb because they have the ability to reduce all but the point of focus to a vague blur. How vague this background blur is can be controlled by depth of field. At f2.8 with a long lens, all but the point of focus will be a wash of colour.

RIGHT
Ed Brown casts at sunset on the La Salinas saltwater flats in Cuba. The sunset colours are gorgeous. The subject has been placed dead centre of the frame to draw attention to the symmetry of the cast. This shot illustrates the importance of controlling the position of the sun in the shot. In this case, the camera position has been tweaked to allow it to peek under the caster's arm. The effect is that it draws the eye into the key subject without swamping the shot and, critically, without creating excessive lens-flare (a sure result if the sun was not

Sometimes, we want the background to be very abstract while at other times we want to see a hint of what it contains but we don't want so much detail that it begins to compete with the main image. In this case, an aperture of, say, f4 or f5.6 is more suitable.

If there is one error that stands out in angling photography more than any other it is poor framing. Anglers, it seems are terrified of not getting the subject in the frame so they 'back off' and use the widest frame possible, losing the subject of the photograph surrounded by distracting clutter. My advice is that get in as close as you dare and frame out anything that is distracting or does not contribute to the image. And when you have tried that, get a shot with an even tighter frame!

Low camera angles usually create an imposing image. The angler and catch will dominate the scene; the action shot will have a sense of urgency and impact. Low camera angles also give more emphasis to the sky and when the sky is interesting this

can be a very good thing. Blue skies pepped up with a polarising filter always look good; moody or angry skies make the scene dramatic; sunsets and sunrises add a sense of calm. High camera viewpoints create a more 'fly on the wall' type feel and are very useful when the sky is flat and uninteresting. On days when this is the case, I always try to frame the sky out because it tends to reduce the impact of the image.

I like high viewpoints when there are bridges, ridges, hills or winding rivers to take advantage of. From waist to head-height camera angles are very natural – this is the angle from which we are used to seeing things. Images taken from this angle can lack the impact of low angle shots but they are very good when we want to stick to the classic formula of preserving the rule of thirds. The differing camera angles are also suited to certain types of lenses. High and low viewpoints usually work best with a wide angle lens while waist to head height viewpoints work best with medium and telephoto lenses.

BELOW
A classic example of a beautiful scene with poor composition. The rock and the boat in the foreground are fighting for the viewer's attention and arrest the eye from travelling through the image. Also, the photographer's shadow can be seen on the right side. This image was destined for the trash but I rescued it to illustrate the importance of two items of equal prominence competing for attention.

ABOVE
This unusual release shot has been framed deliberately to retain the detail of the battered old Cuban skiff from where the captor was fishing. A low viewpoint balances the shot and retains the blue sky, while the use of fill-flash has blown away the harsh shadows that would have ruined this image.

How Camera Angles Affect Images

Low Viewpoints: best taken with wide angle lenses to favour the sky. Create dramatic images with a sense of impact. Human subjects tower over the picture and dominate. Low angle viewpoints are especially good for trophy, action shots and whenever the sky is interesting.

Waist to Head Height Viewpoints: are natural viewpoints and are well suited to 'the rule of thirds' type composition in landscape. They are also very good viewpoints for long lens work, isolating human subjects and capturing action from a distance.

High Viewpoints: create a 'fly-on-the-wall' feel and are well suited, primarily to wide and medium length lenses. These viewpoints work very well on river landscapes and wherever bridges, parapets or ridges/hills are present. They create unusual images and are very useful when the sky is flat and uninteresting.

Whereas composition and depth of field are all about how we portray what is in the scene, framing takes care of what we include and exclude. The basic rule is that what we exclude is often just as important as what we include. In an obvious example, we can frame out distracting objects.

These might include colourful distractions like life-belts, buckets or people other than the main subject wearing bright clothing etc., Bright, colourful objects or high contrast objects (such as a white sign, for example) will draw the eye away from the key focal points in the image. Sometimes a splash of colour can be good – I have seen some great images of anglers wearing brightly coloured caps, for instance. As a general rule, however, be wary of bright objects unless they are the main subject of the image.

At a more advanced level, framing is used to make sure that the viewer sees only what we want them to see. If something does not contribute to an image or is in the wrong place (so that it spoils the composition) frame it out. A classic example is fishing tackle strewn around the bank when you are shooting an action or portrait shot.

ABOVE

This composition is uncomfortable and shows the danger of including a brightly-coloured object in the image that drags the eye away from the main subject. This image could be saved by making a vertical crop to transform it into a portrait shot, cropping out the float and concentrating on the bass in the net.

LEFT

Here is the same fish, photographed next to the bright float and the bait that caught it, a mackerel. This time the image works because the colourful bait and float add punch. The composition is pleasing and looks natural, rather than staged.

RIGHT

My good friend, Mick Brown, fishes for grayling on a very remote river where few have ever cast a line. The high viewpoint, looking down on the river canyon provides a very unusual bird's eye view. The foliage and tree trunk have been used to create a natural frame. 35mm, 1/50th sec, f5.6, ISO200.

Sometimes, if it is placed in the right position, fishing tackle can create foreground interest but if it is cluttered or just randomly scattered it rarely looks good. A good example of using fishing tackle might be, for example, to have a fly box at the front of the image placed to one side of the foreground with the angler fishing in the background. The angler can be in the centre of the frame or on the opposite side to the foreground object but should occupy the line that creates the top third of the image. This is a pleasing composition and one that helps to tell a story. We can see the angler fishing and we know what type of flies they are using.

One of the nicest ways to create a frame is to use a natural object or piece of structure to create a frame within the frame. An overhanging branch can create a beautiful natural frame for an angler casting underneath it. Rocks and bridges are another useful way to create frames that draw attention to our main subject. They place the subject within its environment but are used to draw the viewer's eye toward the focal point of the image.

Finally, a word about lenses because the type of lens you use and its focal length are the features that enable you to frame, compose and choose interesting angles. There will always be a right lens for the image that you want to convey. If you only own a single lens or perhaps a pair of lenses, you must learn to look for the images that suit your equipment.

If you own a selection of lenses you have more options. Knowing how different lenses perform not only in terms of their framing limitations but also how well they react to unusual angles, how close you can get to the nearest subject and keep it in focus, how much the lens compresses distance and how much apparent depth of field it delivers for a given aperture setting, is vitally important.

Zoom lenses are very good for creating frames because as we zoom through the focal length we selectively crop out the distracting parts of the scene. Prime lenses of a fixed length often deliver superb image quality but require the

photographer to move closer or further away to create the correct frame.

Sometimes, however, the discipline of using say, a 50mm lens, will help you to become a better photographer. When you look at a scene, you must learn the art of seeing it in 'frames.' You will learn to see at 14mm, 24mm, 50mm, 100mm, 200mm and 400mm. Only by regularly using lenses at these focal lengths will you develop the intuition of what lens you should fit to the camera to portray the image as you see it.

At the same time you will learn the capability of lenses at different focal lengths and how they react to differing depths of field. Wide angle lenses (those between 14 and 28mm) offer a much greater apparent depth of field over their zoom counterparts and so they are usually the first choice when it comes to landscape. Medium length lenses between 28 and 70mm are very versatile and offer great flexibility with depth of field. Long lenses, above 70mm compress distance and are best suited to shallow depths of field.

Chapter Eight

MACRO, CANDID, WILD AND STILL-LIFE, ABSTRACT

If you are like me, you will realise that not only as anglers do we have unique opportunities to take photographs of things that normal people rarely see but we can begin to expand our photographic horizons to make a day spent fishing even more enjoyable. Some forms of angling take us into some of the most remote and beautiful places on earth; we see wildlife that some nature photographers would love to photograph; we are surrounded when we fish by insects, plants and other micro-organisms that make great photographic subjects; fisheries are often surrounded by interesting objects and textures.

Sometimes broadening our photographic horizons can help to tell a story about our angling adventures or even help us to become better anglers. I have spent a great deal of time, for example, photographing water-borne insects and as a consequence I have been able to incorporate this knowledge into my fly tying. Other opportunities to take images not directly related to the sport just make a day on the river bank more pleasurable, especially when the fish are not biting. I developed a passion for photographing the Northern Lights after visiting Norway. I visited Norway initially just to go salmon fishing. My interest in photography now extends way beyond my sport but it may not for you. Nonetheless, being out in nature at all times of day and night in all kinds of weather offers us some terrific photo opportunities.

Wildlife

I have photographed some fantastic wildlife when I have been out fishing: foxes, water birds, deer and even moose have all been captured by one of my images. Taking good wildlife shots when you are out fishing involves being prepared: expecting the unexpected. We need to be able to have the camera within reach with a lens fitted, when a deer pokes through the clearing, a water bird suddenly takes flight or a pike appears in the margins of the lake with a prey fish clamped across its jaws. Because wildlife is, well, wild it usually means that opportunities to fire off good shots are very limited and spontaneous occurrences.

To take wildlife shots it is advisable to have a long lens. Dedicated wildlife photographers often carry huge lenses of up to 600mm focal length but these are rather cumbersome to cart around on a fishing trip! More practical are telephoto zoom lenses. 70-200mm is pretty much the minimum standard. 75-300mm, 100-400mm are also useful to anglers. An f2.8 lens will be heavier than a regular long zoom lens but deliver better image quality.

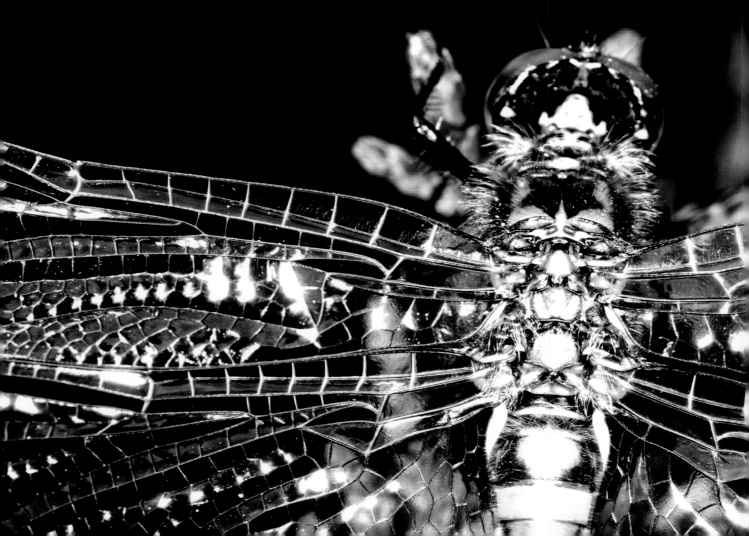

BELOW

A dragonfly is drying its wings after emerging from its nymphal shuck. The process takes over half an hour, allowing me to photograph the creature with my macro lens. I love this detail shot because it shows the intricacy of its wings and the amazing feat of nature's engineering that has assembled it into a flying machine. 65mm macro lens, 1/30th sec at f16, ISO 400, fill-flash.

ABOVE

This action shot of a leaping bottlenose dolphin was captured in Costa Rica. The use of a long lens has homed in on the action and the combination of a wide aperture and fast shutter speed has frozen the moment 300mm lens, 1/3000th sec at f5.6, ISO 200.

I use a 70-200mm lens a lot because it has a maximum aperture of f2.8 which enables me to isolate the subject from its background and because the lens has a much better build capacity than a standard 'zoom', it delivers great results and fast. The lower the maximum aperture of the lens, the faster the shutter speed you can use and the more you can isolate the subject.

Most telephoto lenses have a maximum aperture that changes according to the focal length that they are used at. A typical example is, say a 75-300mm f3.5-5.6. What this means is that the lens has a working range between 75 and 300mm and that at 75mm its maximum aperture is f3.5 and at 300mm its maximum aperture is f5.6. Pro lenses will maintain maximum aperture throughout their focal range – 70-200mm f2.8 being a prime example. These lenses carry a much higher price tag, however. You should also bear in mind that pro cameras with a full frame sensor do not alter the

focal length of the lens: a 200mm will work at 200mm. Most amateur cameras, however, will add 50% onto the focal range. In other words, a 70-200mm lens when fitted to one of these cameras will work at 105-450mm. While this phenomenon can be a disadvantage with wide angle work it is a definite advantage when it comes to the long range stuff.

My advice is to buy the best zoom that you can afford. Ideally, it should be an f2.8 pro or semi-pro model but don't get hung up on it. What is essential, however, is that you invest in support for the lens because most long lenses can only be hand held in very good light. A tripod and or monopod is perfect. Monopods are especially good because they can double as a walking stick and take up little room. Carbon fibre pods are much lighter than any other type. A beanbag is also very useful, not just for wildlife work but also for macro. They are a cheap and simple means of camera support.

ABOVE

This image of a sika looking back is a prime example of the opportunities for anglers to take wildlife shots. I took this shot while fishing at Shatterford Lakes in Shropshire. Note the shallow depth of field to pull the subject out of the confusing foliage in the background. Taken on a 600mm lens, the camera was tripod-mounted to prevent camera shake. 600mm, f4, 1/45th sec at ISO100.

RIGHT

Swans make great photographic subjects. Here I have used a 200mm lens with an aperture of f4 and a shutter speed of 2000th of a second to freeze the water droplets. The backlight helps make the shot. Because the swan fills the frame, there is a danger of under-exposure because the scene is dominated by white. Opening up by one and a half stops from the camera's metered exposure keeps those pristine feathers white. The backlight helps make the shot.

1. **Long lens** - preferably a zoom lens with a minimum focal length of 200mm

2. **Camera support** – either tripod or monopod, preferably carbon fibre construction.

3. **Beanbag** – cheap and reliable, beanbags are also very useful for macro photography.

4. **Lens hood** – the lens hood cuts down glare.

5. **Camera** - with motor drive facility so that it can pile off at least 3 frames-per-second but five or seven are better.

6. **Servo** – this special focusing feature allows you to track moving subjects and lock focus on them. Not all cameras have a servo feature.

Most wildlife photographs are taken at wide apertures. An aperture of f5.6 is just about the maximum but f4 and f2.8 are very widely used too. The wider the aperture you shoot at, the faster the shutter speed will be but remember that an aperture of f2.8 gives a very shallow depth of field. Photographed at f2.8, for example, the head of a deer is 'deep enough' to throw the eyes, nose or ears out of focus, depending on where the focal point is fixed. Head on to the camera, f2.8 would probably be a poor choice of aperture, and f4 or even f5.6 would probably be a better choice. Yet, take the same deer as a full body shot and f2.8 will be acceptable and possibly desirable.

The deer will be in focus but the background will be out of focus. In the same way, the head of the deer, captured side on would render all of its facial features in focus at f2.8 In most situations, when photographing animals, the eye should be sharp. This is because our natural instinct is to look other creatures in the eye and we immediately notice if they are not in proper focus. The same holds true for fish. The focal point of any image including a fish is it eye, this must be sharp or the photograph is disappointing.

Provided that the camera is on some form of support, fast shutter speeds are not always essential. Most animals, when they spot you, will stand frozen to the spot for a few seconds before moving away. If you can capture this moment when the animal is making eye contact you have the recipe for a memorable image. I would be wary of attempting images at shutter speeds lower than 1/60th of a second, however, because any slight movement of the camera or subject will cause blurring in the image.

Sometimes, a very fast shutter speed is required to capture wildlife images. Creatures that are moving will require fast shutter speeds to freeze the action. For animals that are walking, 1/250th of a second is fine; running animals or leaping fish require at least 1/500th of a second to freeze the action.

Freezing the action, while usually desirable, is not always the best. I have seen some fantastic images of birds and animals captured at slow shutter speeds so that they record as an impressionistic blur. It pays to experiment and sometimes a slow shutter speed will produce a less predictable and stunning image. Bear in mind, however, that this form of photography, though simple enough at first glance, takes great skill to execute well.

Obtaining fast shutter speeds when the light is less than perfect is tricky. Often it means switching to a very wide aperture such as f2.8 and switching to a faster ISO setting such as ISO400 or even ISO800. When setting up for wildlife action shots I rarely choose less than ISO200 even in the best light.

So what is the best light for wildlife photography? Well it is not, as you might expect, bright, sunny conditions. Bright sunshine usually creates harsh contrast and creates shadows in woodland areas especially. The best conditions are undoubtedly strong but diffused, even light or low, directional light such as that produced at dawn or dusk. Even lighting avoids harsh shadows and preserves tonal range. This is very important unless photographing wild creatures in silhouette.

The exception to this is photographing leaping fish in open water (note that the emphasis is on open because places with cover produce harsh shade). Because fish have smooth, streamlined bodies without too many protrusions, in bright sunlight they do not tend to display harsh shadows on their bodies the same way that other animals do. I have photographed leaping pike, sailfish and marlin in bright sunshine and obtained good results. These speed jumpers require very fast shutter speeds and I regard 1/750th of a second as the bare minimum but 1/1000th or more is better if you want to freeze the whole action including the fish and the water droplets that spray off its body.

Even the most mundane subjects can make fantastic and memorable pictures. We all take certain water birds like swans, mallards and coots, for example as simply part of the scene. Capture them when they flap their wings or take off, however, and they make fantastic photographic subjects. This type of wildlife photography is all about seeing beyond the normal and waiting for moments. One of my biggest selling stock library images is a swan looking down at its own reflection in the water.

The challenges of wildlife photography are immense. Great wildlife photos require preparation, a sound knowledge of how cameras and lenses work (often shutter speeds and apertures have to be set 'on the fly'), fast reactions and an ability to focus quickly, an ability to frame at lightning speed and patience/anticipation. To illustrate a point, let me tell you about one of my recent projects. It is a good example of practical learning with wildlife imaging

BELOW

I was out fishing on a cold winter's day when this goose appeared. A true character, some of its antics were highly amusing, including turning its head upside down and looking back at me. This is an example of a spontaneous moment when being by the water with a camera pays dividends. 200mm, 1/250th sec at f4, ISO 100.

The Leaping Salmon – a Story of Trials and Tribulations (not to mention pain!)

In the summer I run a salmon fishing lodge on the Gaula river in Norway (lucky me, eh?) Not far from our lodge there is a waterfall located in a gorge. At certain times of the year, Atlantic salmon stack up at the fosse (waterfall) and attempt to jump it. A truly spectacular sight, sometimes there are as many as three or four fish in the air at the same time and some of these fish weigh over 20 kilos!

Getting a shot a leaping salmon is easy. A 200 or 300mm lens from the top of the gorge will produce a useable shot – but not a classic. I wanted a classic. I realised that to get the classic shot I needed to get closer to the action and fill the frame. I wanted a big salmon, in close-up, with a maelstrom of white water behind it. Consequently, I began to visit the fosse regularly, climbing down into the gorge to get closer to the waterfall with over thirty kilos of kit on my back. The climb was perilous and I took risks. Eventually, to get as close as possible to the action, I enlisted the help of my wife's cousin whom is a mountaineer. I had him rig me up with a harness and suspend me over the fosse. I got so close to the leaping salmon that they struck me several times!

As exciting as it proved to be, the cradle was only partially successful. I was close enough to the fish to use a medium length or even wide angle lens but the lack of light in the gorge and the angle they jumped at meant that whereas I could freeze the action I tended to get fish that looked rather dark without any details to their flank colours. I experimented with flash but found that the huge amount of white water made its use detrimental – the water tended to bounce too much light back and not on the side of the flank that I wanted lit!

Eventually I realised I would have to go back to climbing down to the bottom of the gorge and using a long lens. By cheating the angle a little I realised that the flank detail of the fish would be picked out when the odd fish jumped at just the right angle, especially if the light was good (almost always between 1 and 3pm). I now resigned myself to the fact that I would probably only get the shot I wanted when the light was it its strongest and the fish were at their least active.

One of the problems of the fosse is that the salmon will not jump so often in bright light. Only when the gorge was in shadow would the fish jump with enough regularity to make attempting to photograph them a realistic exercise. This meant that, shooting in the shade, even shooting wide open at f2.8 I had to bump up the ISO speed to get the right shutter speed. I found that 1/1000th of a second was pretty much the acceptable minimum so more often than not ISO400 was as good as it got.

I tried photographing the fish with a 400mm lens on a tripod and a 2 x converter from the top of the cliff. The problem was that fitting the 2 x converter converted my 400mm from a 400 to an 800mm lens but it also took the maximum possible aperture from f2.8 to f5.6. This meant that to get fast shutter speeds I had to jump to ISO1000. When I studied the images I found that they were too grainy (digital noise) and I also found that with the converter fitted the images, no matter how hard I tried, were not pin-sharp.

Eventually, using the 400mm lens without a converter from a closer viewpoint allowed me to get sharp and relatively noise free images. However, the salmon jumped so quickly and unpredictably that using the auto-focus was impossible. Rather, I had to focus manually on where I thought the fish might jump to. This was very difficult, especially shooting at f2.8 with a very narrow depth of field. Because the fish were suspended mid-air and therefore not right next to anything I could only use the waterfall or the rocks as a vague reference. Focal points were eventually reached by experimenting and then locking off manual focus when I got some sharp results.

Of course, given the speed of the leaping fish it was no good pressing the shutter when the fish entered frame. Rather, I had to guess where they would reach the apex of their jump and fire the shutter a split second before the fish entered the frame.

Eventually I got some memorable images but this is a prime example of where angling photography can lead you to. To get my shots I had to sacrifice many days of salmon fishing and I had to go through physical pain and danger besides. Would I do it again? You bet!

ABOVE

A large male salmon attempts to clear the raging white water of the Eggfossen on the Gaula river in Norway. Immense patience is required to get shots like this one. With around twenty-five kilos of kit on my back, I climbed down a steep rock face to get to the base of the falls. Using a 400mm lens set to manual focus and a remote release, the shot was pre-framed and focused. After that, it was simply a matter of firing the shutter every time it looked as if a fish might enter the frame. Eventually it al came together and I got this shot. 400mm lens with 2 X converter, 1/250th sec, f5.6, ISO 800.

Angling really does lend itself to experimenting with macro photography. Just about every location we ever visit will offer great opportunities to take macro shots. Items of fishing tackle like hooks, baits, flies, lures etc., are perfect subjects. Both wild and urban angling locations have a wealth of macro subjects from the fish we catch (photographing scales and fin detail) to small plants, leaves and insects. The paint that flakes off the old boat in the mooring, its securing rope or the fungi that grow in the corner of the boat yard might not jump out for your attention, but look at them and by this I mean really look at them and you will realise that they are infinitely beautiful. Even rust and decay can make stunning images.

Of course, there are some classic macro angling subjects: water borne insect such as dragon flies, mayflies and caddis flies not only make fascinating photographic subjects, macro photography teaches us about their shape, form and habits – all of which are valuable pieces of information to any fisher but particularly to the fly-fisher.

MACRO PHOTOGRAPHY
CHECKLIST

1. **Macro Lens** – there are 50 and 100mm macro lenses. The 50mm lenses are probably the best but 50mm lenses deliver great results too. Canon have released a 65mm macro lens that can deliver up to 5 x life size images and it is amazing though tricky to use.

2. **Reflector** – I find a reflector invaluable for bouncing light back onto a subject to produce even, gentle light that removes harsh contrast and shadows. You can make your own macro-reflector out of some simple kitchen foil and it has the added advantage of being very easy to carry!

3. **Ring flash** – macro lenses usually require special flash guns to produce evenly spread light that does not overpower the subject. These are called ring flashes and they are basically rings that fit around the lens. They are invaluable for top-class macro work. I have recently invested in Canon's latest macro flash. It is a special model which, instead of utilising a ring, has two mini flash heads mounted on a collar. The heads can be controlled independently and angled differently. They can also be tuned to give differing flash outputs to produce stunning effects. I have found this flash gun to be a revelation because its ability to produce just the right amount of flash on the auto setting in almost any situation is nothing short of staggering. Used with the 100mm macro lens it also makes a great portrait flashgun.

4. **Support** – some tripods are really good for macro work. They can be assembled so that the centre column can be removed and the camera shifted as close to the ground as is necessary. A bean bag support is also invaluable for hand-held work.

5. **Cable release** – with macro, any form of camera shake can ruin the image. Depth of field is so precise that any amount of small movement will shift the focal. Most macro works requires manual focus with a remote release to avoid the danger of camera movement.

6. **Brush** – a small, soft brush is very useful when photographing plants and leaves – it can be used to brush off any unwanted debris. A human hair or loose seed head can ruin a macro shot.

7. **Spray** – an atomiser spray filled with water reproduces dew and helps to make plants look fresh.

8. **Tweezers** – useful for removing stray objects that the brush can't shift.

9. **Diffuser** – sometimes natural light produces the best macro images and a diffuser of some sort will help to soften the light. I picked up a small, collapsible cube for photographing items intended for sale on e-bay that is great for macro work. I believe these cubes are called 'light cubes.' They weigh next to nothing and fold down so that they are easily transported. Of course, I cannot move plants to put in them but for items of fishing tackle and some insects they are invaluable, producing soft, natural diffused light.

LEFT

This tiny water spider was photographed with a very powerful macro lens. Focusing is critical when attempting to photograph tiny organisms like this - the spider was less than 1cm in size! Certain styles of fishing, such as carp fishing, when there is plenty of time to study your surroundings while waiting for a take, lend themselves to this style of photography. The macro world is fascinating - it is a hidden world that few bother to explore, but for those who do, it is fascinating. This shot was taken with a special Canon Macro Lens that actually magnifies the image and allows photography of subjects from mere millimetres away. A great lens, but one that is all manual focus and tricky to use. A special macro ring flash was used.

BELOW

Here is one of the bees that I refer to in the text. I spent hours of fishing time on a top - and expensive - salmon beat, fixated on capturing an image of a bee in flight. 100mm, 1/250th sec at f5.6, ISO200, flash.

One of the fundamental rules of macro photography is that we do not damage the delicate plants and insects that are our subjects. We should take care and not damage the environment we seek to photograph. This is part of the respect for nature that goes hand in hand with being an angler.

Sometimes this can make macro work really frustrating. Insects are particularly troublesome as they have a habit of not settling where you want them to settle and flying off just when you are going to press the shutter. Focusing is critical with macro lenses and even high f-numbers will produce a shallow depth of field so being patient is a big advantage.

I once broke into a fishing session to photograph some bees that I saw buzzing around some fox gloves near to the river. I followed the bees around, waiting for them to settle and I got some pretty pleasing images. I wanted to get an image of a bee in flight, however, and herein lay my downfall. I became so obsessed with the moment just before they land or take off (this being the only practical time to

get the shot) that I lost track of time. Focus was all manual and had to be very quick. I was constantly changing exposures and flash output as the light went in and out behind clouds. Eventually I began to notice that the light had become rather dull. Without knowing it I had spent more than five hours trying to get that magic image and I had failed to realise that the sun was setting. I had spent a whole afternoon photographing bees instead of fishing!

Great Macro Subjects for Anglers

Here are just a few suggestions to get you started. When you are fishing look around and then look really closely. You will soon discover a world that you never knew existed!

- Fishing flies, lures, hooks, floats, reels
- Waterborne insects such as dragon, damsel, caddis and mayflies
- Aquatic insect larvae (carry a petri-dish)
- Leaves
- Wild plants
- Fungi
- Fish details such as scales, fin rays, eyes etc.,
- Terrestrial insects such as ants etc.,
- Spiders and spider webs
- Dew drops, icicles and frost
- Peeling paint, rust, nails
- Fungi, autumn leaves
- Feathers
- Baits

The best days to macro photograph are days with good light that is even and diffused by thin cloud. Calm days are also essential if you want to photograph plants. Any slight movement will knock a macro-shot out of focus. With insects, photographing them early in the morning is probably the best bet because after a cold night they are usually drowsy and less likely to fly away or run off.

Knowing where to fix the focal point and how much depth of field to employ are the keys to good macro work. Sometimes a very shallow depth of field so that only a very small amount of the subject is in focus can be very powerful. Other times, maximum depth of field is much better to capture as much detail as possible.

ABOVE

A nice shot of a blue-winged olive just after it has emerged. The insect is drying its wings while perched on the underside of bankside vegetation. This is a prime example of what can be achieved with a macro lens, providing not only interesting images but also a useful reference for fly tyers. 55mm macro lens. 1/60th sec at f11 ISO 200.

Even at f11 and f16, most macro-lenses will lift a subject away from its background. Because objects have a habit of moving (particularly insects), when using a narrow aperture such as f11, a burst of flash will help to freeze the subject and keep it sharp even though the shutter speed is likely to be quite low. This is why ring flashes are so invaluable for macro work. Not only do they assist with sharpness, they also give off soft, even light. I regularly combine a reflector with ring flash, albeit with the flash at a low setting. The reflector produces soft, even ambient light while the ring flash kicks in just enough to freeze any movement.

Abstract Images

Abstract images are not everyone's cup of tea but they can be stunning. We are particularly fortunate to spend so much time by water – a source of countless abstract images because it ripples and reflects. The nice thing about abstract images is that you don't need sophisticated kit to capture them. A standard camera kit lens (medium zoom) is often perfect.

Abstract images are basically patterns, shapes or colours that are not immediately obvious. They can often involve deliberate blurring or recording washes of colour. They should give a hint of something that is recognisable but contain an element of mystery. Ripples on the water can form fascinating shapes and contain amazing colours, especially at sunset. I have often been fascinated by the light that plays around a boat wake when I am fishing, for example.

Reflections are perhaps the anglers most pleasing abstract. They can form part or whole of the image. Often, when I am photographing fishing friends I look for reflections in the water. A fish being returned can make a great subject if you isolate it and include its reflection. Medium and long lenses are best suited to abstract work. Generally we shoot with wide apertures and frame out all but the most desirable colours, reflections or shapes. For angler and fish reflection shots I like to compress focal distance and most often use a 200 or 300mm lens.

Movement is another great abstract subject. Giving a sense of movement by using slow shutter speeds is a key photographic technique. The object of the exercise is to allow the viewer to see what the subject is (an angler making a cast, birds taking flight while flapping their wings or grasses blowing in the wind, for example) but to introduce enough blur to create sense of mystery and movement.

One of the trickiest shots you can attempt in angling is an angler making a cast without freezing the action. The trick is to be able to still see that there is a fishing rod being held. Too slow and the rod is lost as a vague blur; too fast and it is frozen in time. The best way to achieve this effect is to use flash and a slow shutter speed combined with a wide aperture to make sure that any distracting background shapes are reduced to a blur. Quite often it is best to fit a polarising filter even when you do not need one to cut down some of the light entering the lens (remember that polarising filters hold back two stops of light). Doing so will allow you to use a wide aperture such as f4 or f5.6 with a slow shutter speed. The ISO setting on the camera will need to be low too – 100 or even less if your camera has a 'Low' ISO setting.

The slow shutter speed creates blurred movement, recording the casting movement as a streak or smudge. The flash freezes enough of the action to sharpen up and semi-freeze part of the casting stroke so that you can see the angler and the rod – though not too clearly. The effect is a shadowy figure casting a rod with a blur of movement behind them.

In order to pull this off, the flash must fire at the end of the exposure – not the beginning. If the flash fires at the beginning of the exposure, the blur of movement will be in front of the partially frozen subject. This is not natural. Think of a car. If the blur is behind the car we can sense that it is going forward. If it is behind it, the car appears to be going backwards. To get the blur behind the angler we must override the flash setting at put it on second curtain sync. At factory default, the camera and flash are set to fire at first curtain sync. In other words, the flash fires the moment the shutter opens. With second curtain sync it fires just before it closes. You should consult your camera and flashgun manuals to establish how to switch to second curtain sync.

You will need to experiment with shutter speeds and flash outputs to gauge the best result with that delivers the right combination of blurred and frozen movement. The flash should be set to manual, not auto and experiment with firing less than full flash and more than full flash until you get the effect that you like. Dull days are best for this type of project. You will also need a friend whom is happy to make repeated casts!

BELOW

Spring has arrived and with it the melting of the ice on the Gaula river. This image illustrates how powerful semi-abstract images can be. The subject is simple - a rock with ice-cold water flowing around it. A close crop ensures that the colours in the rock and the water are the focal point of the photograph. A slow shutter speed of one second has been used to capture the movement in the water and add a soothing abstract touch. The camera was tripod-mounted, 100mm lens, 1 second at f32, ISO 50.

My challenge to you is that you record a fishing trip in images. Having done so, you invite one of your friends to view the pictures, a family member or anyone whom has no prior knowledge of where you went fishing or what you went fishing for. After showing them the images ask them the following questions:

Where did I fish?
What did I catch?
What equipment did I use?
Were there any exciting moments?
How was the weather?
What bait, lure or fly did I use?
Was the trip fun, disastrous, dangerous or challenging?
Did I fish in an ordinary place or an extraordinary location?
Are you inspired to try the same thing?

The answer to all of these questions should trip off the tongue of the person whom you are asking. If they don't, you have failed to tell the story of your angling adventure in images. Moreover, you are not ready to become an angling photo-journalist.

It is possible to fulfil the task by using a compact camera – you don't even need an digital SLR. The point is that you use the equipment you have got to tell a story.
More often than not, it is the fill-in still life images, the stuff that can be a pain in the proverbial to shoot that you have missed out on. It might be the 'Welcome to such and such fishery' sign or the rod with the surface lure attached to it.

How we precisely define 'still life images' is difficult. I guess that I am applying the term to images that don't readily fall into other categories. One of the best examples I can think of here is photographing details. Fish don't have to be large to make great images. Small, colourful fishes, while not suitable for trophy shots nonetheless can be wonderful subjects. So too can the details of fishes – scales, fins, tails, eyes. Often the fins of fish are shot through with colour and they are beautiful to photograph backlit by the sun. To some extent this overlaps with macro photography and abstract but for some of these beautiful shots you don't need a macro lens and a standard kit lens will do.

TOP
Words are not needed to tell you that this is a selection of flies for Belize. A nicely composed shot that provides important technical information and makes a pleasing image. This type of shot is very important for angling photojournalists.

ABOVE
A classic example of a 'still-life shot' of a stunning fish, in this case a 3lb perch. The composition and angle have created a pleasing image and one that is much more interesting than a shot from directly overhead, as is usual in angling photography. 100mm, 1/45th sec at f5.6 ISO 200.

Still Life

These are the shots that can be very useful in telling a fishing story. The fly box, the kettle steaming over the fire, the road sign, the arrival scene, the rod propped against the tent etc., Taking shots that help to fill the gaps in is a key skill if you want to be an angling photo-journalist. Most of us are keyed into the obvious task of photographing fishing scenes, actions and trophy images.

For those of you whom want to make a career or semi-career out of angling I have an interesting exercise for you.

...me images are important and what's more they can be very evocative. A shot of an old kettle, encrusted in burnt enamel and charcoal, a veteran of so many fishing trips, looks great when shot steaming over a real fire. It speaks volumes about you – the fishing veteran of many adventures. It is also an appealing image to non-fishing people and helps to convey a sense that fishing trips are fun and exciting. These are the shots that string together adventures and bring them to life. Don't ignore them, especially if you harbour ambitions to make a career out of angling!

Candid Photography

You don't need special equipment to take candid shots. More often the standard kit lens with your DSLR will be good enough or you can use a compact. Candid refers not to some form of exhibitionism or pornography but to a style of photography of people. Candid shots are the un-posed, unexpected snapshots that capture the mood of the moment. There are plenty of great moments involving anglers and if you can capture them you will succeed in making some memorable images. Typical examples are anglers 'high-fiving' or shaking hands after the capture of a big fish; disappointment after losing a fish; contemplation; determination or any other spontaneous show of emotion. The point is that the shots are unrehearsed and unrepeatable.

Some of the greatest characters I have ever met have been while on an angling adventure. Guides, ghillies and the 'locals' that prop up every bar in every major angling destination in the world are the people I am referring too. These are the people with craggy, grumpy faces: faces that looked lived in and tell a thousand angling stories without them even having to open their mouths. These people beg to be photographed. Converting the images to black and white in post production is often a good idea because most great character studies look better in monotone than colour.

Needless to say, it is one thing to shoot when people are off guard but you must seek their permission to use the images. Also, never attempt this type of photography if you think that it might cause offence. I did so once while in the Caribbean and I ended up almost being accosted by my photo subject, a man whom had deep religious beliefs. His religion taught him that taking a photograph of another human being was an attempt to steal their soul. While there is a funny side to this, it is not funny to cause genuine hurt or offence. What I am saying here is to use your sense and suss out situations and atmospheres before you attempt this type of photography. Also respect the privacy and beliefs of others.

BELOW
I have enjoyed so many adventures with regular fishing partner Mick Brown. We had spent the night in Mick's camper van on the banks of the river Avon in Warwickshire. We woke at dawn to find that the landscape and margins of the river had frozen overnight. Candid shots like these bring back a lifetime of memories. 40mm, 1/250th sec, f4, ISO200.

Chapter Nine

ANGLING PHOTOGRAPHY AT THE LIMITS

I am one of those anglers fortunate enough to have travelled all over the planet in pursuit of my lifestyle. I have been fortunate to visit some of the most inspiring places that anyone has ever cast a line in. In the early days I was so keen to experience the wonderful fishing that photography took a definite back seat. Nowadays, taking pictures in awe-inspiring angling venues has become more important than what I catch.

There are others who feel the same. I have enjoyed conversations with fellow angler and photo-journalist, Henry Gilbey. Like me, Henry got invited to foreign fishing destinations as a consequence of being a TV angling personality. At first he was just as captivated as I was by the fishing but nowadays he is dedicated to taking images of angling adventures to the point where he fishes on these trips for just a fraction of the time. Henry's images are very, very good and he is getting better at photography all the time. He is a prime example of an angler so affected by the shutter bug that it has changed his life and re-shaped his career. With youth on his side and a growing talent, he is going to be one of the great angling photographers of all time.

My own lifestyle allows me to indulge my passion for exploring new forms of angling photography in world class destinations. I do not travel as much as I used to because I have a young family. I still go on occasional long trips, however and I have the added bonus of living half the year in the UK and the other half in Norway where, with my wife, I run a fishing lodge on the banks of one of the world's great Atlantic salmon rivers, the Gaula.

Norway is a truly inspiring photographic location with its amazing scenery, extreme weather and unusual light. Despite having lived on and off in Norway for more than five years I have only just scratched the surface of the amazing imaging opportunities that it has to offer. I have recently taken on the new challenge of shooting some film using the movie function of my DSLR camera and I am enjoying the new challenge enormously.

They say that travel broadens the mind and this is certainly true in my case. I have gone beyond simply capturing angling images and I now spend some of my time photographing landscapes. Capturing images of the northern Lights or Aurora Borealis has become one of my passions. The point is that the travelling angler has a unique opportunity to portray adventures in images and will only truly succeed if those images tell not only what the fishing is like but also what the place, the atmosphere, culture and people are like.

ABOVE

Dawn breaks on Lake Storsjoen in southern Norway. The soft mist gives a subdued, slightly eerie feel to the image. The red cabin in the foreground adds a nice splash of colour and the eye is led from the cabin along the mist-shrouded shoreline. A panoramic crop is perfect for pulling the eye through the image. Angling provides wonderful opportunities for landscape photography and capturing nature at her finest.

Not that you have to travel to indulge in extreme photography. Heat, cold, rain and wind are part of nature and extremes of weather are experienced by all anglers all over the world on a regular basis. How many of us have not fished in a major thunderstorm, wind or snow storm or rain-lashed landscape?

The natural instinct of anyone with expensive camera gear is to put it away in these conditions and rightly so but there are occasions when the opportunity for a quick 'grab shot' comes up and these should be grasped with both hands. I was out fishing for carp once in a full solar eclipse. I sincerely regret not being into photography at that time – what an amazing event! I saw the classic eclipse moment – the diamond ring – and I can clearly remember that in the period of around two minutes that the earth went dark, the birds stopped singing and the

atmosphere was like at a football match when the crowd is asked to observe two minutes silence. Fortunately I have seen and photographed a full lunar eclipse since. I would love to photograph a full solar eclipse.

I was once trapped in Havana, Cuba during a hurricane. Despite being locked in the hotel by the local authorities, I was literally busting to get out and take some pictures as soon as possible after the event. I managed to sneak out for half an hour before being rounded up again and I got a few shots that showed the chaos caused. I once also photographed a large water spout in Cuba (a sort of mini tornado) chasing the flats skiff that my friend Ed was fishing in. Sadly it was a bit of a grab shot that I screwed up in post-process and since I don't have the original file raw file I can't have another crack. The shot conveys the drama of the moment though.

BELOW

Believe it or not, this is spring fishing! The venue is the partially frozen Folla river in Norway. Here, Bjornar stands on an ice sheet to cast a fly for grayling that are feeding sporadically on the first hatch of stoneflies. The action is frozen using a fast shutter speed. The low viewpoint helps the caster to dominate the scene, while the receding ice sheet makes a good lead-in line. 24mm, 1/250th sec at f5.6 ISO 100. Note how the wide-angle lens delivers a greater depth of field than a long telephoto.

There is no escaping the fact that extremes of heat and cold can cause huge problems for a DSLR camera. Because they are based around electronics (unlike the literally bullet-proof reportage cameras of old) relying so little on mechanical functions, they are prone to failure in wet or damp conditions. Ice and snow cause huge problems not just with battery life but also with lenses and buttons freezing up. Beaches are terrible places for cameras: the sand gets into everything. On a recent trip to Mozambique we camped out on a remote island right on a stunning beach. If I had not carried a soft paint brush in my kit, enabling me to brush off the sand (that even managed to penetrate the layers of my camera bag), I am quite certain that my camera would have stopped working. Indeed, I have lost several camera bodies and lenses to extreme conditions in the past.

Camera insurance is very, very expensive – especially if you take it overseas. I partially insure mine and gamble on the premise that I will not destroy all of it at once. Needless to say I have learned to take care of it.

RIGHT
Mozambique is certainly one of the hottest and most difficult places I have ever fished and taken photographs in. This is Hell's Gate at dawn and Wes Peens is casting a popper for GT's. I love the way the beach snakes off into nowhere - it sums up the remote atmosphere of this unusual place 16mm 1/80th sec at f11, ISO100.

STANDARD KIT FOR EXTREME PHOTOGRAPHY
(not including lenses)

Pro or semi-pro camera body (these are more resistant to moisture and dust

Back-up camera body (just in case)

Plug adapters for battery chargers
Spare Batteries

Flash gun and Spare Flash Gun

Special rucksack/camera bag with water proof seal

Blower and paint brushes (for cleaning and dealing with sand

Lens cloths

Cloths for wiping away excess moisture
Remote release

Silica gel sachets in camera bag (to soak up excess moisture)

Polarising filters

ND filters

Head Torch and spare torch

Carbon fibre telescopic tripod

Lens tissues and lens cleaning fluid

Arctic butterfly sensor and mirror cleaning brush/sensor cleaning swab kit

Rain Cover

FOR COLD COUNTRIES

Extra clothing for survival
Gloves

'Bubble-wrap' (to wrap around camera to keep out the cold)

Hand warmer heat sachets (to strap to camera to prevent it from freezing up

Rain Cover

After the photo session in either extreme cold or heat I find that the Lowepro kit bag I carry is a god send. It has plenty of padding, a bullet proof construction and it has a water proof seal. The extra seal and protection flap, in addition to providing protection from water ingress, will allow the contents to warm up and cool down slowly. If I am taking shots in sub-zero temperatures, for example, I find that if I take the kit bag out of a warm environment and into the cold air, provided that the kit bag is zipped it will cool down slowly. I take the kit out into the cold for an hour prior to removing the camera from the bag and when I have finished shooting, I put the camera back in the bag and zip it up. I have found that taking the bag back into a warm environment causes no problems with condensation because the camera warms up slowly. I have not had a camera malfunction because of sudden or extreme temperature changes since using this kit bag/rucksack.

The most important tip that I can give you about photography in extreme environments is to clean your camera kit after every session. Start by dusting away any sand with a soft paintbrush. Wipe down lenses with a damp cloth and do the same with the camera body. Next, wipe round the lens contacts to remove any salt or grit. Finally, remove the lens and use a blower brush on the mirror. Check each lens and, if necessary, brush off the front element and use a lens tissue and liquid to clean the glass. Clean the sensor at least once every trip (this is a tricky operation and should be thoroughly researched before you attempt it).

There are limitations to the amount of kit that can be carried on an overseas trip. Thanks to the worldwide terror threat, travelling with camera kit is now a bit of a nightmare. Before you travel, always check and re-check the baggage restrictions. I never put camera kit in the hold – I have seen the way baggage handlers behave (including the USA and the UK) and it is a disgrace. Baggage is treated with a level of disrespect that I find astonishing and the only place I have seen it treated respectfully is Scandinavia. The reality is that your camera kit needs to go in the overhead locker on the plane and that means using a bag that is of an acceptable size and making

hard choices about what lenses to carry. Some of the kit, such as flashguns, battery chargers, tripod and cleaning kit etc., can be packed in your regular baggage.

Typical Lens Selection for Overseas Trip
16-35mm f2.8
28-70mm f2.8
70-200mm f2.8
100mm macro

Armed with these four lenses I can cover just about any photographic situation and whilst I sometimes miss the selection of lenses I used to take pre 9/11 at least carting them around is easier! Obviously, if going on a photo-safari where wildlife is going to be more prominent I would look to take a zoom lens with a longer focal length.

enough to have taken photographs at the very extremes of heat and cold. The hottest place I ever took a photograph was Phoenix, Arizona in the middle of July. It was so hot that when visiting an Indian reservation one day (to take a look at the Snake River) that my feet were burning through the soles of my sneakers! The coldest I have taken photographs in was minus 27 while photographing the aurora borealis in Norway. Eventually I had to stop taking shots because the lens on the camera began to ice up but having packed hand warmer sachets and bubble wrap around the camera body I was delighted that the Canon IDS MK3 that I used to take the shots carried on working perfectly!

equipment that lend themselves to extreme photography. The first is a polarising filter. In hot or tropical countries the skies can be spectacular and a circular polariser will deepen the blues and bring white clouds into sharp definition.

A range of graduated Neutral Density filters are also very useful if you intend to do any serious landscape work.

Because I spend a lot of time on boats when I am adventure fishing, I have found that a wide angle lens is very useful. In boats that have limited space, a wide angle lens allows the photographer to get up close and personal.

BELOW

The aurora borealis appears over the ridg flanking the Gaula river, Norway. This shot w taken as the river began to freeze up for th winter. It is twenty below, a challenge for camer equipment. Getting the aurora is fair straightforward, but how to light the river? exposed for the northern lights and then with a off-camera flashgun, fired the gun repeatedly light the river and snow. 16mm, 47 seconds f2.8, ISO400.

BELOW
This panoramic image was created by stitching together four shots in Photoshop. It is early morning; the bay next to Kilchurn castle is a mirror, reflecting an image of white-topped mountains, powder blue sky, and the ancient stone castle. Eric and Tiny Hope drift through the bay, casting lures for pike. Being in a boat myself, I had no choice but to handhold the camera and try to keep the frame as constant as possible while I tried a range of shots, panning across the scene. I knew that this image would make a great panoramic and I was really pleased with the result. A polarising filter was used to deepen the blue in the sky and saturate the wonderful colours. Images like this come along once in a lifetime. 28mm lens, 1/125th sec at f6.7, four images stitched together in Photoshop to create a panorama.

LEFT
Waves pound the Maecon in Havana, Cuba, in the aftermath of a hurricane. While this trip was almost a write-off in fishing terms, it provided the opportunity for a great travel image. This is a classic example of photography adding another dimension to the angler's lifestyle.

we all love to take photos in boats, especially those shots that show the team speeding out across the water on the cusp of another adventure and a wide angle lens is the one to use. I love to experiment with camera angles for this kind of shot and I have achieved some nice results while holding the camera over the side so that I can shoot along the hull.

A long lens is also a necessity. There is always something to see in the distance whenever you are fishing in new places. A long lens will also help you to capture those spectacular sunsets. I have seen some amazing sunsets in the states, Africa and the Caribbean where the sun has been literally a huge ball of fire at sunset. These moments beg for a classic silhouette.

One of the things that I have noticed while on my travels is that the sky is always different from continent to continent. In Britain, an overcrowded country that the government seems hell-bent on making even more over-crowded, the light pollution is horrendous. I was staggered to see that the night sky really is deep blue, just as it is depicted in paintings and cartoons, when I went overseas. I was amazed and I must say slightly overawed to realise that compared to England, where the night sky is black with a hint of dirty orange, I could see ten times as many stars.

Scandinavian skies are clear. Of course there are cloudy days but when the sun is out and the sky is blue it is a deep, deep blue. It begs to be captured and sometimes it is so blue that a polarising filter sends it such an improbably blue colour that I leave it off.

In Caribbean countries, Australia and the Keys, the sunsets are to die for. The sky is awash with spectacular colours, especially if there is just a scattering of cloud to 'anchor' it. I also found the sunsets in Patagonia amazing – I was desperate to see one of those red 'mackerel' skies while we were there and on the last night we got one.

Despite the fact that we were on one of the best, if not the best, sea trout rivers in the world, I simply had to put the rods down and photograph Steve, my fishing partner and guide, Diego, until we could no longer see in the darkness!

In Ireland, on the West coast, I love the golden afterglow after sunset. I once looked at a Val Atkinson photo that had a literally yellow/golden sky and I was dubious about its authenticity, suspecting a 'Photoshop job.' That is, until I saw some of those Irish gloaming periods on Loughs Corrib and Mask and I realised that this is a regular phenomenon.

ABOVE
For the whole of my week at Argentina's Rio Grande, I had waited for one of the legendary sunsets. I had already caught my dream fish and the photography took over. 16mm 1/200th sec f5.6 ISO 200.

LEFT
Late afternoon light rakes across the Rio Grande in Argentina. A black and white treatment in postproduction, using a red filter, has given this image an infra-red film feel. Images of this type are eerie and slightly haunted, a mood, I feel that matches the desolate nature of the landscape.

I am led to believe that there are some pretty spectacular Autumn colours to be enjoyed in parts of the USA and I would certainly like to see them one day but I have seen fabulous autumn scenes both in Scandinavia (where in addition to the trees, the whole ground can go red, orange and gold) and in England's Lake District. The English Lake District along with the Devon coast are pretty much the only unspoilt parts of England left and I must say that I treasure every visit I make to them, especially in the Autumn.

Extreme photography is not just about climates and weather patterns, seasons and skies, however. Those of us whom travel regularly do so to catch big or unusual fish that we can't catch at home. It doesn't matter whether you are travelling half-way around the world to Christmas Island to fish for bonefish or taking a short trip across the channel to catch a big carp or catfish, the point is that you should be ready to snap the fish of a lifetime. Never is it more important to ensure that the other members of your party can handle the camera if you get that fish-of-a-lifetime. One of the first jobs I undertake with a new guide is to give him a quick tour of how my camera works.

Of course, there are some places where fish jump. With the exception of pike, sea trout and salmon we don't have so many sport fish in the UK but the ones that we do have make great subjects. Pike are among the most underrated fish in the world. Arguably because of their widespread distribution, they are the world's greates[t] sport fish but it is a sad fact that they are persecuted almost everywhere. I love photographing leaping pike, whether they are hooked on fly, lure or bait and I have some great shots of them. Every spectacular shot, however, has been taken while no [one is] actively fishing. To photograph jumping pike it is best to fish from a boat. I use a 28-70mm lens set to f5.6. I like a shutter speed of 1/1000th of a second, so I tweak the ISO setting through 100, 200 and 400 until [I] get it. Pike have a habit of head shaking when they hit the surface and they often shake in mid air. There is a lot of movement and it needs to be frozen. I always add a burst of flash for good measure, just to freeze the action and capture the spray from the water droplets.

ABOVE
A Costa Rican sailfish explodes from the water, scattering water droplets like diamonds. The focus is spot-on in this pin-sharp image and a fast shutter speed has frozen the magic moment.

LEFT
A 20lb-plus pike, hooked on Ireland's Lough Ramor, explodes on the surface before taking to the air. I was ready for this shot with the camera already set at a fast shutter speed to freeze the action. To get shots like this requires a willingness to put the rods down and pick up the camera - although spontaneous, moments like this benefit from preparation. 70mm, 1/2000th sec, f4, ISO 200.

RIGHT
This shot shows the extremes I have been driven to by my passion for angling photography. To get into position, I employed a mountaineer to rig me up in a harness and lower me down the wall of the rock face. I got my shots but I was struck by leaping salmon six times!

Of course, there are other fish that are spectacular jumpers. I have been told that sturgeon jump a lot but I have never bothered to fish for them. I have, however, fished for three of the world's most spectacular jumpers – sailfish, marlin and tarpon.

Sadly, most of my fishing for these species took place before I got really serious about angling images and whilst I attempted to photograph them I was too hooked on the fishing and not experienced enough to make a good job of it.

Since then, i have obtained some very nice shots of sailfish particularly while I Costa Rica and I have photographed leaping tarpon in Cuba. I must say that I am very keen to return to the Florida Keys to photograph tarpon midair.

I know from my own experience that the camera's meter is always fooled when trying to take jumping fish shots. This is because the reflectance of water rarely matches the sky. I have found that the only way to get good shots of leaping fish is to shoot with the camera set to manual – even AV mode does not quite cut it.

Photographing Leaping Fish

1.   Ideally you will set up two cameras – one for the long range stuff and another for close-range work, if the fish leaps close to the boat. If you are restricted to one set-up choose the one must appropriate to where you expect the fish to jump. Marlin, sailfish and tarpon will usually jump most when well away from the boat, so a long lens set-up is advisable. You can change lenses as the battle approaches its climax. For pike, trout and bass, a shorter lens is usually fine as they will jump close. My long lens will be a telephoto zoom, say 70-200mm or 100-400mm. The short range lens will be a 28-70mm. Flash can be useful on the short range set-up.

2.   Make sure that you do not have a polarising filter fitted but do fit a lens hood to cut down any stray glare from the sun and to protect the lens from spray.

3.   Set the camera to manual and dial in an aperture of f4 or f5.6. This should deliver sharp results (at f2.8 it is difficult to get all of the fish fully in sharp focus).

4.   Now set the shutter speed at 1/1000 of a second or even greater if the light is strong.

5.   Fire off a test exposure of the water and/or the horizon.

6.   Is it too dark or too light? If underexposed, shift the ISO setting up through 160, 200 and up to ISO400 until you get a well-exposed image with a fast shutter speed. This is a process of trial and error.

7.   You will need to be alert for any changes in light conditions. If it gets brighter, drop down the ISO speed, if the sun goes behind clouds, up it (usually by two stops – i.e from 100 to 400).

8.   Constantly monitor the light values and remain. Fish often jump just after the moment of hook up.

9.   The camera focus mode should be servo. You will be using the autofocus. In servo mode, as long as you keep the subject in the centre of the frame and the shutter button half depressed, the focus will lock and track moving subjects

ABOVE

This salmon leaping on the Gaula river almost hit my lens as it tried to ascend the waterfall. The focus is manual and preset. The firing of the shutter requires split-second timing and the ISO speed has to be pushed to 250 to deliver a shutter speed fast enough to freeze the action. 78mm 1/2000th at f2.8, ISO 250.

TOP RIGHT

A pike takes off, standing on its tail as it explodes from the water shaking its head. Shots like this do not happen by accident. The exposure and flash setting were dialled in before the fish was hooked. 70mm, 1/1000th sec, f4, ISO 800.

RIGHT

A silver-bright fish leaps at Eggfossen, Gaula river Norway. The point of focus is critical; the focal point was set manually along with aperture and shutter speed. The timing of the shot is perfect.

Focusing and shooting in servo requires practice.

10. Always try to look up periodically when the fish is one the line. Be constantly alert for where the line meets the water. Ask the angler to tell you if they think that the fish is going to jump. You will see the line noticeably cut up through the water just before a jump.

11. When the fish appears press the shutter button all the way and keep it pressed down until the fish re-enters the water.

Modern DSLR's perform very well at high ISO settings and I have achieved good results with ISO's set as high as 800. This breakthrough in low light performance has been achieved in recent years and cameras are getting better and better at shooting at high ISO settings. Whereas I will always try to shoot at the lowest ISO setting that I can get away with, the most important thing with leaping fish is to freeze the action.

Photographing leaping fish is something you get better at: anticipating the jump, tracking the moving subject and capturing those magic moments takes practice. With this game, you have to kiss a lot of frogs to get a prince. Not all jumps are the same and out of 100 jumping fish shots you might have 20 good ones and 10 really good shots. Four or five will be classics. The way the fish jumps – whether you see back, flank or belly, its position in the frame, how much it fills the frame, the light on the fish etc., are all important factors in sorting out good images from great images.
.
Another key point to bear in mind is the sharpness of the image. I have taken good photographs of fish where, because of the angle of the jump, the whole fish is not pin sharp but the eye should always be visible and it should be sharp. I don't know why it is, but a leaping fish image where the fish's eye is not visible just does not quite work. There may be exceptions to this rule but the only ones I can think of are large billfish that leap vertically, exposing their back to the camera.

Boats are difficult places to take photographs from but they are interesting subjects. I am constantly on the lookout for other fishing boats when I am out fishing, especially if they move across the sun. Another interesting technique to try is to shoot another boat moving at high speed if it moves parallel to your own boat. Provided that the boats are moving at a similar speed it is possible to get some great 'blur pan' shots without having to 'pan.' 'Panning' involves moving the camera while taking the shot.

A blur pan is used to shoot racing cars and motorbikes whereby the photographer moves the camera to keep pace with the vehicle. Get it right and the background is reduced to motion blur but the vehicle or bike is sharp and in focus. Boat to boat, there is little need to pan but the effect is very similar. Alternatively, try the blur pan technique from a slow moving or static boat or from land if you see a fast moving boat approaching.

The other use that I can think of for the blur pan technique in angling photography is to pan with an angler making a cast. Use a low shutter speed, a burst of flash and experiment! Another possibility for those anglers whom camp out a lot is to try the technique with water birds. When territorial, swans often scoot across the water flapping their wings to scare off other birds. Many species of water birds skim across the water just before take-off.

Panning with these subjects can produce interesting abstract results. I have yet to try the technique with leaping fish (opportunities to photograph them are so rare that I always opt for the classic freeze-frame shot) but I can quite imagine that the results might be very nice, especially with a fish that is making flat, 'grey-hounding' leaps.

How to Blur Pan

1. Set the camera with a wide aperture of f4 or f5.6

2. Auto focus or servo modes for focusing should be active.

3. Dial in a long exposure – 1/30th of a second down to ¼ of a second is good.

You will need a relatively long exposure to get the blurred background effect.

4. Pan the camera, keeping the subject either in the centre or to one side of the frame. Subjects that are moving look better if they are moving into space rather than out of it. If the subject is moving left to right, therefore, it is better on the left side than the right.

5. While keeping pace, fire the shutter several times.

Using flash in extreme angling photography is not always possible. It relies on the main subject being close enough for the flash to illuminate it. Shooting against water can cause problems with the flash bouncing back, especially if the water is white. Nonetheless, a burst of flash will help to freeze moving subjects if you can get close to them.

There are two possibilities here, the first being to shoot with a relatively slow shutter speed so that there is some blurred movement while the burst of flash freezes the subject and creates whereby the subject still looks focused and relatively sharp but there is motion blur around it.

ABOVE

This shot of my pal, Ed Brown, casting, shows how dull, stormy weather can provide memorable photo opportunities. With a polarising filter fitted to the lens (to cut some light back), I was able to use a slow shutter speed (1/25th sec at f8) in the middle of the afternoon. The slow shutter was accompanied by a burst of flash to freeze some of the movement associated with the cast. The unusual look of the image was created by zooming the lens during the exposure. The flash was set to manual and tweaked to kick out just the right amount of light. 35mm lens, 1/25th sec at f8, ISO 160.

RIGHT

Tierra del Fuego, sea trout capital of the world, is famous for its big, fiery sunsets and open landscape. After catching my dream sea trout on the Rio Grande, my attention turned to photography and I was rewarded when, on the last night, the heavens caught fire and fishing partner, Steve, and guide, Diego, fished on until the last colour had bled from the sky. A very careful amount of fill-flash was used to light my subjects and a controlled exposure, to maximise the drama of the sky, made for tricky imaging but the results were worth it.

For this technique, second curtain synchronisation of the flash gun is important. I have already described second curtain synchronisation when describing the creativity photography of casting in the previous chapter under 'abstract images.'

When using high shutter speeds there will be relatively little, if any, motion blur but a burst of flash can add a little extra 'zip' to the image. You will need to consult your camera and flash-gun manuals if you want to use flash at over 1/250th of a second. With good flash guns, this is possible but you will need to understand how to activate the high speed flash sync.

Of all the forms of adventure angling photography, fly fishing probably offers the greatest opportunities. There are several reasons for this. Firstly, the process of casting a fly is one of angling's most beautiful images. The movements are graceful and the line is clearly visible. Secondly, fly fishing seems somehow more natural and in-tune with nature's rhythm. Fly fishing images somehow look more harmonious with the natural environment than any other form of angling. Finally, most forms of fly fishing take place in dramatic scenery.

One of the nicest images you can capture is of a fly line uncurling on the forward stroke. Needless to say, you will need to recruit the services of a good caster whom can create effortless tight loops to do this. You will also need to position the caster so that the line will be seen against a dark background: storm clouds and dark tree lines offer the best possibilities. The best images will be obtained by shooting the moment the fly turns over at the end of the forward stroke.

Double hand casting with a spey rod is another great subject for angling photography. This is arguably the most visually beautiful form of the sport. From a photographer's viewpoint, speycasting is a dream. Capturing the loops of line that are formed in the various types of cast from single spey to snake roll is challenging but well worth the effort.

In short, extreme angling and adventure photography is about pushing the boundaries and taking images in conditions or places that few photographers get to visit. While it is easy to get swept away by the power of nature or the grand scale of scenery, we must never forget to look for the details. Sometimes it is the detail shots that truly capture the enchanting nature of angling: the bonefish tail; the colourful starfish; the ice on the flap of the tent; the fly box on the sand. And sometimes it is about photographing the angler in his/her element: a small figure casting in a towering, powerful landscape.

Chapter Ten

UNDERWATER PHOTOGRAPHY

This chapter will be relatively short because by no means am I an expert in sub-aqua photography. This being said, I have owned several underwater housings for cameras and I have developed a passion for photographing fish in their natural environment and particularly for fish being returned to their natural environment.

Modern technology has put basic underwater photography within the grasp of all of us. There are now compact cameras that are submersible to several meters that, in addition to taking nice stills, will also take movie footage. Carrying such a camera is a great idea for any angler, even if their preferred medium is a digital SLR.

For a couple of years now I have been using the Panasonic Lumix FT3 camera and its predecessor the FT2. It is a compact camera that features quality optics and it is a powerhouse for its size since it is able to capture 12 mp stills and quality video. The camera is submersible and it works well underwater - even the flash can be fired when it is submerged. And while it won't deliver the very best

underwater images it does a creditable job. For anglers looking for a great camera on a budget, at the time of going to press, this would be my pick of the bunch.

interesting underwater or semi-submerged images can be captured with Go Pro cameras. They come with an underwater housing and can be used to shoot both regular and timelapse stills as well as HD video. These fun cameras can be strapped to your head or chest or mounted on poles if you are boat fishing and want to capture some interesting catch return shots. On the bank or wading, they are small enough to be held in your hand and simply pushed underwater. The latest version, the Hero 2, captures amazing footage and images for a low price.

For those of us whom are more serious about underwater imaging, a purpose-built housing for a DSLR is the way to go. My latest underwater housing, to fit a Canon 1DS Mk 3, was supplied by Cameras Underwater in Devon. They gave me plenty of good advice about which housing to choose (there are several manufacturers) according to the needs I described.

RIGHT
Fishing aboard a boat from Crocodile Bay Lodge on the Pacific coast of Costa Rica, Peter Collingsworth displays a beautiful sailfish. I took this shot while in the water using an underwater housing. I treated the front of the lens port with silicone solution so that the water would drain off it quickly.

BELOW
Another powerful image that speaks volumes for angling conservation taken with a dedicated underwater housing. For shots like this, clear water is a must and the crystal depths of the Tya river in Norway are perfect. 16mm, 1/100th sec at f5, ISO 400.

The housing has a large dome port at the front and I use it with a 16-35mm wide angle lens. It offers full functionality of all key controls, having sealed extensions that manipulate the dials and buttons on the camera. It also has twin strobe flashes, attached via two side arms, enabling me to experiment with lighting.

Though I only ever use the housing at depths no greater than a few feet, having the flash facility has been a great benefit. And, needless to say, being able to use a top quality lens means that the images I can obtain are stunning.

The biggest enemy to underwater angling photography is water that is anything less than crystal clear. Sediment is an enemy – it is a nightmare if you try to use flash and whenever it is present you will experience huge focusing problems. I am very fussy about where I use the housing but provided that the water is clear I am happy to experiment in salt and fresh water and in both rivers and lakes.

Perhaps my most unnerving work with an underwater camera was while in Costa Rica. While photographing sailfish and rooster fish releases I was very aware that the water I was swimming in is inhabited by more or less all of the world's most dangerous shark species. While photographing billfish, I was over very deep water, several thousand feet deep and, when I looked down and saw the water change from pale blue through every shade until it turned indigo, I experienced a form of vertigo. Nonetheless, the images I obtained were memorable and I would do it again in a flash.

RIGHT
This image of a pike chasing a lure was shot with an underwater housing. I got lucky - pike had been following lures to the boat all day - and by simply hanging the camera over the side of the boat, and firing off a few shots when I saw fish following, I hit the jackpot with this image. 16mm, 1/200th sec at f5.6, ISO 200.

Perhaps my favourite underwater subjects are bonefish. They inhabit shallow, crystal clear water, often accompanied by white sand. Such places are a dream to photograph and I have numerous memorable images. My favourite is an image I got of a Belizean bonefish chasing a fly while I was hanging the camera over the side of a skiff. The bonefish was so fixated on a fly that had been dropped on its nose that it was oblivious to the boat and the pair of hands dangling the big dark camera housing almost within touching distance.

I have achieved similar results when predatory fish 'lock on' and follow lures or flies right to the boat.

Of course this is not always possible but it is still feasible to capture the moment or at least the essence of it. The way to do it is to take a snap of a fish being released. It must be a clean shot with no hands or other parts of the human form in the shot. Next, you must immediately take a

photograph of a lure r fly being dragged in front of the lens. This is to ensure that the lure or fly are lit in the same environment at the same time. After this, it is simply a matter of clipping out the fly or lure and pasting it in Photoshop onto the image of the 'chasing' fish. Provided that the fly or lure has been shot in the same light and location it can easily be blended in. A little bit of motion blur applied to the lure will add to the shot.

No doubt many of you will regard this as nothing short of 'cheating' and I agree that achieving the image by Photoshop is nothing like as rewarding as capturing the real thing. But the chances of doing this are very, very slim and would require a lifetime's work. What we are doing when we create these shots is to construct the image so that we can portray what happens underwater. And since, in many cases, there is no other way of getting these shots without making the fish suffer I think that they have their place if they are well executed.

ABOVE

A classic underwater shot of a bonefish. The fish has just been released but good framing and timing have made this shot look entirely natural with the tip of the fish's tail poking through the surface film. The framing and angle of the subject add to the impact and the presence of the turtle grass places the fish in a classic environment.

RIGHT

A roosterfish is released off Costa Rica's Pacific coast. To get this shot I used a dive housing and risked attack from some fairly nasty sharks known to be in the area!

One of my passions is to take shots of fish being released back into their natural environment. Despite the huge advances in catch and release being made worldwide there are many countries in the world where killing game fish is not only accepted but encouraged. I regularly speak at seminars and angling shows about catch and release and 'minimum foot print' angling and these release shots sum everything up perfectly. Contrast a fish being released back into crystal clear water with an image of a dead fish being paraded by its grinning captor. The emotion generated by the two images could not be further apart. One suggests an exploitation and disregard for nature while the other portrays respect for both quarry and environment.

Taking good underwater images involves both luck and judgement. Looking through the viewfinder is not easy when wearing goggles or facemasks and in shallow water the housing is most usually lowered into position by a wading angler. A wide angle lens will allow you to get close to the subject (a fish, lure. fly or rig) and it is usually a matter of pointing the camera and firing off some shots. Moving the camera around and trying different angles is a good idea. I also like to use some fill flash to add a little bit of extra light,

pattern and sharpness. You cannot use a built-in flash in most underwater housings so extra strobe flashes are required.

I always set the camera to auto focus because the subjects I photograph rarely stay sill long enough to use manual. Most of the time I am either photographing fish that have been lowered into the water, released, or they are free swimming. Auto focus works pretty well underwater provided that the water is clear and though it can occasionally lock focus onto the wrong thing, provided that you are pointing at the fish and the visibility id good, it is right more often than wrong. Focusing problems will be experienced when there is sediment in the water which is why I try to avoid it (this and poorer quality images). The lens will hunt for a focal point in water that is carrying colour or sediment. Flash will exaggerate sediment in the water and make it look worse than it is.

The setting I favour most in camera is an aperture of 6.3 with an ISO setting at 200. The camera is set to AV (aperture priority) and,, having dialled in the aperture, I let the camera figure out the shutter speed. Occasionally, in evenly lit water, I will revert to manual but AV does it for me most of the time.

The angle you shoot at can produce interesting effects. Side-on to the fish produces the most reliable images but head into the camera (but not directly so) with the lens pointing down the flank of the fish looks good too. Shooting from a low angle toward the surface is nice too because it usually produces a perfect reflection of the fish or the fish being held in the captor's hands on the surface of the water.

Setting the flash is not a major problem. I have found that the strobe flashes I use are very good at measuring the amount of output required to produce a natural image. Occasionally I experience problems but this is rectified by switching the flash over to manual and backing it off.

Perhaps the trickiest shots to get are the 'half and half shots.' These are the shots where the camera gets an underwater shot of the fish either on the line or being released and the angler above. Usually the water comes half or two thirds up the frame. To get this type of shot you must choose the right day – a day with lots of sunlight and deep blue skies. Nothing else seems to work because the light underwater has to match the light above as closely as possible.

If this is not so, the camera exposes for one or the other half of the image and the result is either under exposed underwater or over exposed above the water. Burnt out skies is a problem with this photography because the camera tries to expose correctly for the underwater part of the scene and since the sky is brighter it ends up white in the image. It is possible, of course to fire off two shots in quick succession at differently bracketed exposures and then merge the sky and the underwater scene in Photoshop. My policy is to frame out the above the water element unless, of course the conditions are suitable.

When conditions allow, 'half and half shots' are very memorable and well worth chasing. There are other problems to deal with, however. Getting a level horizon is trickier than you might think. Also, any waves or ripples on the water will encroach on the lens port and many shots are ruined by an uneven water line that obscures the above the water element of the shot. A wide dome port on the housing helps enormously with this problem and is the perfect partner to a wide angle lens.

As the years pass I am becoming more comfortable with and more keen on unlocking the full potential of underwater imaging. I have even used the housing to photograph rigs, flies and lures to get a fish eye view. The information I get back is always invaluable. In the future I hope to do more underwater work, particularly with brown trout and salmon. One of my 'dream' images is a trout photographed underwater rising to take a fly off the surface. Now there's a challenge!

RIGHT
This shot of an Atlantic salmon being released was taken on the Gaula river, Norway, using an underwater housing and strobe flash. Such specialised kit has limited use in angling photography, but for the addict can lead to exciting opportunities to capture images that sum up the magic of angling. 16mm, 1/30th sec at f5.6, strobe flash set manually at 1/32nd output

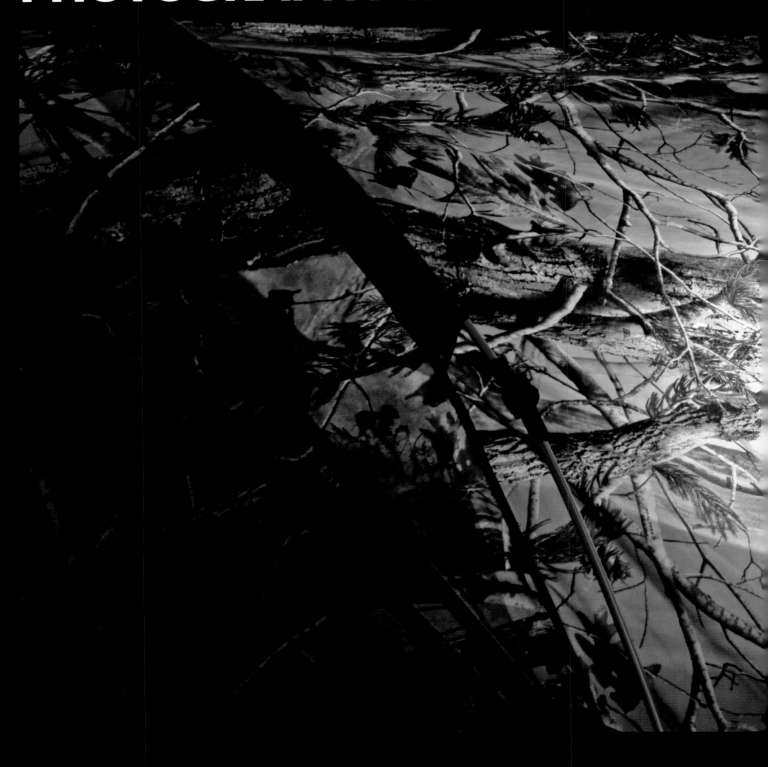

Chapter Eleven

NIGHT AND LOW LIGHT PHOTOGRAPHY IN ANGLING

Night-time imaging is one of my passions but it is not something that we generally associate with angling photography. Yet, since a lot of fishing goes on at night, the potential for night-time photography is enormous. The world changes at night and takes on a totally different appearance: familiar places become unfamiliar; unfamiliar places become enchanting, if not a little scary sometimes.

Night fishing and photography is not for everyone. I find the hours of darkness fascinating, mystical sometimes and this passion is reflected in many of the night images I create. Some people, however, find the dark rather intimidating. It is a time when creatures stir. Animals rustle around in the undergrowth; bats flit on leathery wings; shadows appear to shift. Yet, by the same token, the night is extraordinarily beautiful, especially those clear nights when the water is still and the lake is a mirror, reflecting a canopy of millions of stars. Some countries and locations lend themselves better to night photography than others. The United Kingdom is poor for the star canopy night shots because it suffers from excessive light pollution but by the same token artificial lights can look good in night images. Bright lights on the distant shoreline add a colourful splash to the photograph; boatyards and industrial settings that often look rather ugly in daylight can look captivating in the dark because of the combination of lights and the structures. Needless to say, calm, clear nights are always the best.

From a technical viewpoint, night photography is tricky and requires preparation and a sound technique. It also lends itself to experimentation because when the lights go down, the rules of photography change.

RIGHT

This shot of the aurora borealis was taken while on a cod fishing trip to Northern Norway. The art is to use a wide-angle lens, manually focused on infinity. The depth of field with wide-angle lenses is much better than with telephoto lenses, meaning that shots like this are made wide open at f2.8 and f4. The art is to get a long enough exposure to get the colour in the sky, but short enough to retain shape in the aurora, avoid blur caused by the stars moving and avoid digital noise. A high ISO setting is essential but this is no longer the problem that it used to be, as the modern generation DSLRs have superb high ISO performance. The white balance is set to tungsten to give the characteristic 'blue' nighttime feel. 16mm, 30 seconds, f2.8, ISO 800.

BELOW

Richard Lee prepares for night fishing for catfish at Burton Mere on the Wirral, Cheshire. A tungsten white balance gives the image a blue cast to emphasise the nighttime feel. An exposure of 15 seconds at ISO 400 has been used. Shots like this, with long exposures, require the use of a tripod.

Needless to say, not being able to see very far makes focusing very tricky. A head torch helps here, of course but I often focus by using the focusing scale on the barrel of the lens. Most good lenses have these and they have markers that allow you to move the focus ring on the lens according to the distance from your main subject in meters. If you focus using the head torch, switch the autofocus on, point the beam of light at what you want to focus on (hold the torch in your hand to do this) and when focus has locked on, take your finger off the shutter button and lock to manual focus. This way the focus will not shift when you make and exposure.

The majority of night images involve the use of long exposures. For short night exposures, up to 30 seconds in duration, the regular functions on the camera will cope. A bulb setting on the camera (this setting allows you to lock open the shutter for more than 30 seconds) is essential if you are serious about night photography as is a remote or cable release. Cable releases enable you to fire the shot without touching the shutter button. Any exposure that is more than 1/10th of a second is likely to suffer from camera shake even when it is mounted on a tripod if you press the shutter button. Very long exposures of 10 seconds or more suffer far less but nonetheless it is easier to use a cable release and avoids the danger of moving the camera during shutter release and shifting a carefully chosen frame.

RIGHT
This river Lea weir pool is so beautiful on a clear night that I wanted to capture its magic. This is a self-taken shot, set up on a tripod. Flash was not used. Instead, I remained as still as possible for the 16-second exposure. I chose f8 to retain some detail in the water flowing over the weir sill, and to keep the structure of the bridge in focus. I was delighted with the result. It was shot on a 16-35mm lens at ISO 800 and an exposure of 16 seconds.

ABOVE
*Wesley Peens poses with a blacktip reef shark
caught off the beach in Mozambique. Rather than
use the camera and flash on auto, I set both to
manual. An auto-exposure would have resulted in
the background being blown out to black with
probable over-exposure of the white shirt and the
white underside of the shark's jaw by the powerful
burst of flash. By using a reduced flash and fill-in
light provided by a lantern, the result is a much
more balanced exposure that retains the beach
detail. 1/60th sec at f5.6, 35mm, ISO 200.*

Low light photography begins after sunset. It is the period that commences at twilight when the sky still has deep colour but shutter speeds are measured in seconds rather than split seconds. When the sky turns deep blue and the first stars appear it is still possible to record some twilight colours – exposures will up to ten seconds plus. In night time 'proper,' exposures will be ten or fifteen seconds or more even when the aperture is 'wide open' at f2.8 and the ISO speed set to 400 or faster. In the middle of the night, at f4, the ISO setting will be eight hundred and the shutter speed will vary from 30 seconds to one minute. Of course, narrower apertures, such as f8 or f11 will necessitate longer shutter speeds of several minutes and so too will dropping the ISO setting below 500.

Shorter exposures using flash for short range subjects can be made but the detail of the night sky will be lost and anything other than the area illuminated by the flash will be rendered black (except light sources, of course). At night, ambient light is still present it is just that it is at such a low level the human eye cannot perceive it, except perhaps on moonlit nights. A camera is different: leave the shutter open long enough at night and the image recorded will look like daylight. The sky will be different, however, with the stars record as 'rails' or streaks of light because the earth is spinning on its axis. Capturing 'star rails' is a well known photographic technique and it produces beautiful images with a surreal quality. To get star rails, the shutter should be open for fifteen minutes or more.

Half an hour is better. Pointing the camera toward the pole star will ensure that the star streaks are circular in nature while keeping the camera horizontal, rather than pointing upward, will create curves streaks.

You must be aware of the effect of recording both the stars and the moon in night images. If you want star rails leave the shutter open for long periods but if you want the natural canopy of stars, keep the exposure under two minutes. The moon 'moves' by its own diameter every two minutes at night and exposures longer than forty five seconds will record the moon as a smudge. In fact, to record a proper moon in the image you need to shoot it separately and 'Photoshop' it in. The reason for this is that the moon is so bright that long exposures simply reduce it to a patch of bright light.

The correct exposure for the moon varies between 1/250th of a second and 1/500th depending on aperture and ISO setting! It is acceptable to shoot the moon, enlarge it slightly and position it in the image using Photoshop layers. When attempting this, however, it is important that you take a range of exposures in an attempt to match the colour of the sky in the main image. Failure to do this will result in the moon looking as if it has been 'cut out' and stuck on the image (which, in fact, it has!) I suggest that you study Photoshop techniques thoroughly if you intend to attempt this kind of image.

The Moon and Stars at Night

Full Moon
ISO100 f4 1/250th
Half or part moon
ISO200 f4 1/125th - 1/250th
Stars, canopy
ISO 400 f4 1 minute
Stars, star Rails
ISO 200 f11 30 minutes

The above settings are a rough guide only.

BELOW
This shot shows just how much detail can be teased out of a camera raw file. The shot has been subjected to minimal postproduction, but the recovery slider in Lightroom has been pushed to its max. It has allowed the detail in this amazing moon halo to be captured perfectly. This shot was taken while sea trout fishing one night. 100mm, 1/8th sec at f3.2, ISO800.

When shooting images at night the biggest danger is digital noise. It is possible to leave the shutter open for several hours but ultra-long exposures are very prone to digital noise. It pays to never drop below ISO200 and I generally stick to apertures no longer than f11, more often using f2.8, f4 or f5.6

The recent releases of pro cameras by Canon and Nikon feature incredible low light performance with ISO settings into the tens of thousands. We are moving closer to the day when it will be possible to get a useable result with a camera hand held on a dark night. Certainly, the massively enhanced performance of these cameras at high ISO levels is going to shorten our nocturnal exposures. More importantly, the traditional enemy of night photography, namely digital noise is becoming a problem of the past. The next decade will see a boom in night-time photography and the results will be both astonishing and thrilling to seasoned insomniac photographers

whom have suffered all the problems that this specialised form of photography has associated with it.

Modern wide angle lenses, especially the pro-build models made by Canon, Sigma and Nikon have remarkable optical quality. When shooting night scenes as opposed to portraits or close-range material only, I set the camera's focus to infinity (check the lens barrel and line up the infinity symbol) with the shutter wide open at f2.8 or f4. The apparent depth of field is excellent and almost infinite. This fact, coupled with the huge advances made in high-end ISO performances in recent years has really opened up the potential of night photography. Any vestiges of digital noise can now be eradicated in post-production using noise reduction software.

A tip I can give you for night photography is to change the white balance setting from daylight or auto to tungsten. This creates a slightly blue

BELOW

I wanted to capture the magic of a carp run in the middle of the night and after setting the camera on a tripod I waited until I got a real take before firing the shutter. To make the alarms more visible, I used a small LED torch to 'paint' with light by waving the light from the torch along the edges of the alarms. The shot involved a long exposure of 30 seconds to capture the movement in the right-hand indicator, and to capture some of the ambient light. By the time I'd lifted the rod, the carp was halfway across the lake. but it is an large water with no snags so there was no danger to the fish. 50mm lens, 30 seconds, f11, ISO100.

RIGHT

I was fishing on the river Wye for pike with friend Martin Duffy when a freezing snowstorm struck. The storm arrived so suddenly that we were unprepared. This is a classic example of a 'grab shot' that captures the drama of one of angling's 'moments.' I had to pack the camera away quickly afterwards - the air turned so cold that our gear was literally blast frozen!

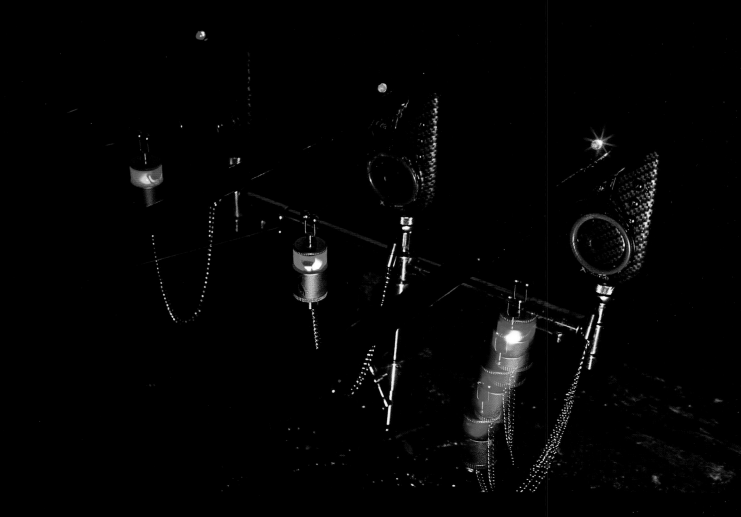

last but produces very faithful night images that look more natural. In the movies, night scenes are often heavily filtered with blue to exaggerate the blue coloured light that we associate with the darkness. Movies are often shot with plenty of lighting even in the dark so that we can see what the actors are doing. When the scene is quite heavily lit, the blue light tells us that it is dark. We can make use of the same effect by using long exposures that make the image lighter than it really is. I have taken long exposures at night, particularly on moon lit nights, that look like daylight. The tungsten white balance provides that important blue coloured night maintain the nocturnal feel.

Most night-time photographs tend to be 'set-pieces' whereby you set the camera on a tripod and attempt to shoot a landscape or angling scene that captures the magic of being by the water at night using a long exposure. There are some exceptions. I have photographed anglers fly casting at night when shooting features about sea trout, for example but flash guns popping near the water are the classic recipe for scaring all the fish in the river! I have also photographed objects in silhouette against the moon such as rods and reels propped against a tent and backlit by the moon. These are the exceptions, however and shooting camp fire scenes or tents and fishing rods are the usually subjects. There is something magical about camping out under a canopy of stars and images of this type have a magical quality. It is possible to include people in these shots but only if they have the ability to keep very still. Adding a burst of flash to the subject will help create a defined rather than a ghostly image.

Moving objects create interesting effects with night photography. The fact that the shutter is open for several seconds, sometimes several minutes, means that anything moving is recorded as a streak or a blur. Carp anglers can use this to great effect by taking slow exposures of bite indicators that have been fitted with isotopes rising and falling when a fish takes the bait; because the earth spins, the stars record as streaks or concentric circles if you point the camera directly

up at the pole star; fireside scenes are surreal and lit by dancing flames.

The final night time photography technique you should know about is 'painting with light.' This is where a flash gun, not mounted on the camera but hand held and fired manually, can be used to 'light up' people, foliage, a tent and fishing equipment. Start by setting the shutter open for between 30 seconds and several minutes. The bulb setting on your camera is used for this. With the shutter open you can begin to 'paint' light. When using flash for this technique, it is best to use repeated bursts at a low output to build up the effect rather than powerful bursts than tend to light the scene unevenly. Hold the flash gun in your hand and set it to manual, preferably at a low output such as 1/8 or 1/16. Next, fire the gun once

or several times over different parts of the scene. You can walk around and do this, pointing the flash gun at different parts of the scene. Use the gun more on some parts of the scene that you want to receive more light, particularly the main subjects.

This technique lends itself to experimentation and you should view 'test' exposures to perfect your technique. The same effect can be achieved by painting light with a head torch. Simply wave the light from the torch over objects in the scene. The more you wave the torch over objects in the image the more light they will receive. This is a very creative technique that lends itself to experimentation – the same is true of all forms of night time photography and that's what makes it so interesting. Have fun!

Chapter Twelve

SOFTWARE, FILE FORMATS AND HDR

I do not intend to give a technical guide to how post-production photo software works because the software is always changing and it is best that you view the manufacturers' tutorials. I can, however, tell you about the software I find most useful.

The type of software you invest in will depend on how serious you are about your photography and what type of imaging interests you. Graphic designers and film makers tend to have heavier software needs than photographers.

Robert Plant of Led Zeppelin fame once commented to a friend of mine when discussing a contemporary band's lack of talent that 'you can't polish a turd..' When I first discovered photo software I could not help playing around with it and looking at the way it changed photographs I had taken. Like many people, I was attracted to the gimmicky software that made the images look surreal, painted or different. I was certainly guilty of over-saturating images and using snazzy filters. Now, when I look at some of the images I ruined by using such techniques I wonder why I ever bothered. The truth is that while software can improve an image, you cannot turn a bad photograph into a good one.

Over the years I have become obsessed with trying to get the image right 'in camera' rather than in post production. And while I do make some 'tweaks' and there are a few filter techniques that I like to use occasionally, more often than not I restrict my post production to levels, curves, saturation and sharpening tweaks to generally improve the impact of the image. Since I shoot camera raw, this is perfectly acceptable and raw files are designed to have these tweaks made to the file. in recent years I have also experimented with HDR of high dynamic range to create images that display a range of tones and colours that gives them an almost surreal look. Yet as I write, HDR software is improving all the time and producing more natural looking images ad well as the 'cartoony' photographs they were initially associated with. More about this shortly...

Let us deal with file formats now. When you take a photograph with a digital camera, the information gathered by the sensor is converted into a file. The file contains all of the information needed to show on a screen or print what you see in camera. All digital cameras do this.

There are really only three file formats that angling photographers should be interested in. The first is J-Peg. This is the format that most photographers use.

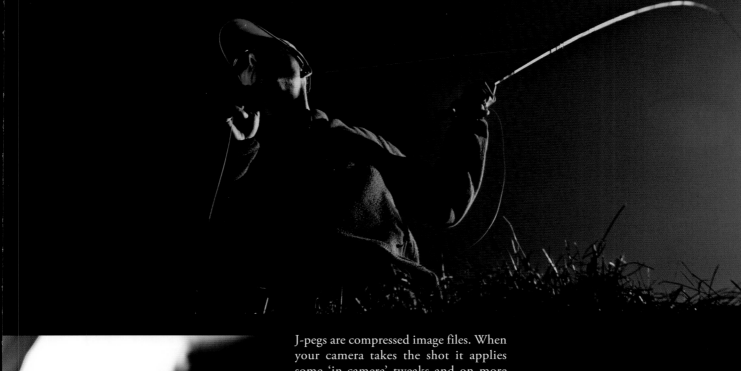

J-pegs are compressed image files. When your camera takes the shot it applies some 'in-camera' tweaks and on more advanced cameras the user can create several pre-sets that control the type and effect of those tweaks. The camera will sharpen, saturate colours and apply contrast as you programme it to. Find the 'parameters' mode on your camera and you will be asked to apply settings for colour saturation, contrast and sharpening.

You can have as many of these pre-stored parameters as you like and you can, for instance, use different settings for your j-pegs when taking action shots, landscape or portrait. This is sensible. Portraits, for example, will look better with parameters that give subtle skin tones and do not apply excessive contrast. By taking the same shot using different parameters, you can see how it affects the image. The advantage with J-Peg is that it takes up less file space than the Raw format, so you can store more pictures on the card. The images require less work in post-production too. The disadvantage is that J-Peg is a compressed file format – meaning that some information contained in the image is discarded by the camera in making the file.

ABOVE

A very dramatic shot that works really well in black and white. The low viewpoint creates drama and the highlights created by the use of a reflector leave an air of mystery, revealing a shadowy form. This is a prime example of setting a shot up and then asking a friend to press the shutter. 34mm, 1/125th sec at f8, ISO100.

LEFT

This study of a brown trout being released was treated to a post-process in Nik Color Efex known as bleach bypass. The process mimics a technique applied to film in which the image was 'bleached' to remove some of the colour and to increase contrast. While it does not work with every photograph, used selectively it can produce strong images with a 'raw' feel. 1/125th sec at f4, 200mm lens, ISO 125.

Without doubt, J-Pegs look better straight out of the camera but raw files invariably trump them when digitally mastered by someone experienced with post-production imaging software.

Most professional photographers and keen amateurs use a file format called camera raw. Once the province of 'pro' photographers, shooting in 'raw' is becoming increasingly popular to the point where some compact cameras now offer a raw file option. Camera raw is a pure, un-compressed image file with no tweaks applied to it. Compared to a j-peg it looks rather flat and uninteresting because it is not sharpened, saturated and has no contrast tweaks made in camera. Camera raw files are designed to allow the user to apply the saturation, contrast and sharpening. When these tweaks have been made, camera raw images burst into life and often look better than their j-peg counterparts. Since the files are not compressed, they take up more space on the memory card and fewer of them can be stored at the same time. They are also time-consuming to process.

The final file format you should be interested in is 'tiff.' This is a file format used for camera raw images after you have carried out the tweaks in post-production. No information is discarded and the image can also carry information about how, when it was shot and what settings were used in camera to get the shot. The process is to tweak the raw image and then convert it into a tiff format for saving and file sharing.

RIGHT

At the end of a day's fishing on a Norwegian fjord, the boat is pointed to the dock, leaving behind a wake that swirls and ripples with colour. Holding the camera over the side of the boat with the focus set to manual, and a 'guess' at a level horizon, captured the magic of the moment. I love the low viewpoint and the surreal, abstract colours. Due to the varying tones and contrasts in this scene, shooting in camera raw really paid off, allowing me to tweak individual elements to create the effect I was looking for. 24mm, 1/125th sec at f5.6, ISO 200.

SOFTWARE FOR...

J-Peg versus Raw Files

J-Peg Pros – takes up less space on memory card, produces better looking images straight out of camera, less time spent in post production, easy and fast format for most devices and computers to read

J-Peg Cons – not the ultimate file format in terms of detail, more limited tweaks can be applied in post production without breaking up the pixels, not the ultimate quality in finished image

Raw Pros – ultimate file for post production, no information discarded, much more flexible in post production techniques

Raw Cons – large files take up more space, time consuming because they require post production, need special software and moderate skills to process them

My preference is for Raw file formats. Despite the fact that they take up much more post-processing time, I like ultimate control over how the image will look. I like to control and apply as much contrast, saturation and sharpening as the image needs. J-peg files can also be tweaked in the same way but since some 'in-camera' manipulation has already gone on and because some of the detail in the image has been discarded in making a file, there is much less latitude than with raw files.

There are several popular post-production software packages, the best known of which is Photoshop. The full version of this software package is truly amazing and its potential for image editing and image creation is almost limitless. As photographers, we only use a minute proportion of its total capacity. While most pro-photographers will buy the full version of Photoshop, its developers, Adobe, have recognised that amateur photographers only need certain elements of it. The result is the superb 'Elements' software that contains all of the essential photographer's tools featured in the full version.

Photoshop contains all of the key features required to make photographic adjustments from raw file conversion, through cropping, sharpening, contrast and various filter effects.

RIGHT

This shot of Lake Windermere was taken from the grounds of my favourite hotel, Cragwood House. To capture the huge range of tones in the image I chose to make three exposures, spaced two and a half stops apart and then merge them in Photmatrix to create a High Dynamic Range image. HDR is becoming more popular among photographers, but care should be taken when processing images as they can look rather 'cartoon-like' if over one. HDR software is becoming more advanced, and natural images with a full range of tones, like this one, are now possible. 63mm, f16, ISO50, three exposures merged in Photomatrix.

BELOW

After tying these flies, I decided to experiment with photographing them. Composition is very important with shots like this one and I spent a long time positioning the flies on the piece of driftwood that they are displayed on. The crop and balance of the shot is important, as is the lighting. Here, I used a modelling light (desk lamp with daylight bulb fitted) and dual flashguns both angled to bounce light off white reflectors to remove any shadows and soften the contrast. I processed three shots and merged them into a high dynamic range image to capture the subtle tones and textures.

t is such an amazing programme that it would be pointless to even try to give a whistle stop tour here. What I will say, however, is that at the heart of Photoshop's genius is the ability to work in 'layers.' Layers are like layers of cellophane laid on op of an image. They allow you to make changes to an image without permanently changing it. Each layer can be made to nteract with all the other layers that contain various additions and adjustments to the base image or they can be made to nteract with only a proportion of them.

The result of this dynamic is an almost nfinite repertoire of image editing techniques. My advice to you is to begin with Elements, learn how to use it and then, if you have the need and desire, move up to the full version.

Another one of Adobe's latest innovations and 'must have' products is Lightroom.' While Photoshop is designed to appeal to all kinds of maging interest groups, Lightroom really is a photographer's tool. With each new version it adds new features, ncluding some very, very good image editing software to add to perhaps the

ultimate image storage and management system in the business. Most photographers do not need any other package than Lightroom and in some respects it is making Photoshop less and less necessary except to designers. What Lightroom does brilliantly is to store and sort your photographs, allowing you to tag them with keywords, organise them into categories and collections, make slide shows, prints and even edit the images. You can, for example, tag any files with the colour red in them with the word 'red.' If you then search 'red' files it will display them. Yet these same files can be organised in more obvious categories such as 'fly', 'salmon' or 'river Gaula.' You can organise by date, by venue, subject or any combination of these.

Collections allow you to make and share collections of images with others. You can even rate images using a star system. Tagged to each image is information about where it was taken, with what camera, what lens, the focal length, the exposure, aperture and whether the flash fired. The photographs in this book were organised in Lightroom.

Before handing them over to the design company, I assigned captions and keywords to each image, dropped them into files by chapter and exported both images and their keywords/data to the designer...

Lightroom is a very powerful piece o software and the one that I use to manage, present and share my files with others. Recent improvements to its image editing interface have made it a more complete package fo photographers. Its raw file editing facility is the best that I have used – better than Photoshop. It also contains some very useful features such as noise reduction and a series of controls to remove chromatic aberration (unsightly bans o colour that appear as 'halos' around part of the image). Both of these feature work very, very well and I am becoming more reliant on Lightroom with every new software release.

While Lightroom contains auto modes to get the most from it, it pays to experiment with its collection of tools, al of which are useful to photographers and none of which are frivolous.

This image of my fishing partner, Ed Brown, climbing out of a salmon pool located in a deep gorge in central Norway lends itself to a gritty black and white treatment. The composition, using the rock face in the bottom third, the angler in the centre and the waterfall in the top third, is classic. The shot has depth and impact.

BELOW

This shot was taken at the end of a day's cod fishing on the Trondheimsfjord, Norway. The lighting on the engine makes this shot. In the middle of the day, the image would be dull and uninteresting but low, directional sunlight and a moody sky transforms it. I have used a toning technique in postproduction to give the photograph a fiery colour cast.

Printing can be carried out via Photoshop or Lightroom. Of the two, I prefer to use the latter. The print interface is very simple to understand and will produce very high quality prints when the output device is a high quality printer.

Other software manufacturers have recognised the domination of the genre by Adobe and as a consequence there is some other superb photo-imaging software designed as a 'plug-in' either for Photoshop or Lightroom. This basically means that the product is installed into Photoshop and Lightroom and becomes part of that image editing package. These third-party pieces of software offer some quite nifty filter and effects packages. My favourite is Nik Color Efex, a very useful collection of filters and photo effects that are based around technology called 'U-point.'

This is basically a very easy to use and highly sophisticated selection system that allows you to apply the effect or filter to selected parts of the image. The package includes graduated filters, polarisers and a whole host of image 'edits' that are used in professional design and glamour photography. There are also Nik products to manage noise and sharpening (DeFine), colour (Viveza). With each passing release of the software, Nik improve the control you can have over the image.

Thanks to U-point, effects can be applied either universally to the whole image or to very specific parts of it. Its ability to make precise intelligent selections and apply filter effects with an amazing level of control is staggering. In the most recent releases, filters can be mixed and matched making precise control over the way the finished image looks possible. Nonetheless, while I use Nik software selectively and almost always subtly, the fundamental tweaks to my raw files continue to be made using Lightroom and Photoshop.

Nik also make another superb piece of software called 'Silver Efex' which is a black and white image conversion software, enabling you to reproduce just about any type of black and white photo effect – it even has an option to mimic the grain found in classic black and white films and features the same U-Point technology to control the effects of one or more filters to every part of the image. Different types of black and white filters can be mixed and matched across the same photograph.

Since most photographers enjoy printing their work, it makes sense to invest in the best printer that you can afford. Printer models seem to change faster than high street fashions and I would advise consulting the guides to printers that regularly appear in leading photo magazines. I have used both Epson and Canon and found them both to be excellent.

To ensure that your prints match what you see on the computer screen , I strongly advise that you calibrate your monitor with your printer. Poorly adjusted monitors (and even when calibrated, they drift after time) will mean that you are editing your photographs with the wrong colours displayed, effectively ruining the image. To ensure that you are seeing the image with its true colours and to ensure that your prints will match what you create on screen, specialised calibration software is needed.

RIGHT
Dawn breaks, revealing stormy skies. A lone boat trolls for ferox trout after spending a night lashed by rain on the lake. A graduated ND filter was used to keep the detail in the sky while allowing a fast enough shutter speed to expose the boat and yet avoid motion blur. This image has been treated to a single image process in HDR Efex Pro to create the drama in the sky, with the original exposure of the boat and water blended into the final image. 1/30th sec at f5.6, 34mm, ISO 200.

This is a High Dynamic Range shot, made by taking five exposures of the same scene and then combining them in Photomatrix. The effect is quite powerful, combining the dramatic, moody sky with the white landscape. The effect is slightly surreal and this is the type of image you either love or hate. 50mm, five exposures, f16, ISO 50.

RIGHT

RIGHT
This is a high dynamic range shot, made by taking five exposures of the same scene and then combining them in Photomatrix. The effect is quite powerful, combining the dramatic, moody sky with the white landscape. The effect is slightly surreal and this is the type of image you either love or hate. 50mm, five exposures, f16, ISO 50.

The best I have found is called 'Color Munki,' a package that includes a special device that makes it possible to produce a very accurate match between screen and printer output. There is a basic monitor calibration package on every new PC or Apple Mac but to get the best results, the specialised software really is worth the money.

One of the biggest movements in post-production software is HDR or High Dynamic Range. This is software that will merge several exposures of the same scene to create an image that it is currently impossible to capture in camera. Inevitably, when an exposure is made, some of the highlight and shadow detail is lost, simply because an exposure is always a compromise that tries to balance the different reflectance of mid-tones, shadows and highlights. HDR is achieved by taking a range of exposures, so that detail in all the key areas is retained. The exposures are then 'fused' together to create a 'super exposure.' Whilst I believe that this will ultimately be achieved in-camera, for the time being this software is very useful to have. HDR has received a mixed reception among photographers because the early images had a very surreal, almost 'painted' quality. When first seen they are stunning, but after a while they can begin to look 'gimmicky.' Thankfully, developers such as Photomatrix and Nik

are now producing software that offers a choice of image effects, ranging from the 'painterly' type through to more natural exposures that look like traditional photographs but simply contain a lot more detail.

In the most recent release of Photoshop, the HDR features have been re-vamped and are impressive. So too is the most recent release from Nik, 'HDR Pro.' The result is software that is capable of producing much more subtle and natural-looking HDR images that raise less eyebrows among serious photographers.

HDR images are fun but they also represent one of the true breakthroughs

in imaging, namely the ability to create photographs that contain an infinite variety of tones that are impossible to obtain from a single exposure.

HDR images are invaluable when you attempt to capture scenes that contain variances in reflectance of the subjects and objects in the scene such as skies, water, land, foliage etc., in unusual light conditions. Shadows on part of the landscape, for example will make creating a balanced exposure when there is bright water or a well-lit sky in the same scene. With HDR we take several exposures to capture the full range of tones, exposing each frame to favour either the mid-tones, shadows or highlights. In post-processing, HDR takes the best elements

of each of these exposures to capture a single image that has a huge tonal range. Moreover, the amount of detail that is often lost in shadow areas or blown highlights is recovered.

At the time of writing, I have just discovered that one of my predictions for the future of digital SLR's appears to have been at least partially fulfilled, namely that sensors will capture HDR images in camera. The new Canon 1DX contains a new feature that allows the user to take bracketed exposures and the camera will then process them to produce a single exposure that captures a great deal more detail. Quite how good this 'in camera' HDR is only time will tell but it seems we are now on the road to HDR coming of age from its rather gimmicky beginnings to the state of the art. This, coupled with the staggering low light performance of the latest generation of DSLR's is redefining some of the traditional boundaries of photography.

I store my images on an external hard drive and I back them up regularly to a second drive. Since most of the images I shoot are at least 100mb (megabytes) in size and I keep copies of both the original raw file and the editing tiff file, the implications of storage are enormous. I find that external drives are invaluable for keeping your PC or Mac running at high speed (do not clutter it with images!) and since they now cost so little money it is easy to buy a pair of hard drives and keep everything in duplicate. I have suffered a hard drive crash twice in recent years and believe me, it is a heartbreaking event. Thankfully, I managed to recover the images on both occasions but on the first occasion it was very expensive.

Finally, we should consider the question PC or Mac. For me, it has to be Apple Mac. I couple my Macbook Pro with a large cinema screen display that allows me to see very precise photographic detail. Working on two screens also enables me to drop the image on one screen and the photo editing tools on the other. This makes working on images much easier and more pleasurable.

I also get the benefit of being able to run slideshows for friends and play them back on the cinema screen. I have also recently started using an iMac with extra ram memory for my post-production work with both stills and movies. Ram or random access memory is very important when working on large image files or film clips.

I find that the Apple Mac is faster and easier to use for anything to do with images or movie files. Originally, Macs were designed for designers and their speed and ease of use in image editing gives them my vote every time. Photoshop and Lightroom seems to work hand-in-glove with Macs. When you buy a Mac you also get the 'i-movie' feature, a very easy-to-use facility that enables you to create dynamic slide shows, mini-movies or a combination of both and add soundtracks, including music.

My addiction to everything Mac has been completed recently by the purchase of both an iphone and an ipad. Using 'cloud' technology, I can share my images between devices in different countries and constantly carry a portfolio of my images with me. Using Mac tv, I can deliver interactive slide shows on large tv screens that mix stills with graphics, stills and movie clips, all set to music. And of course, I can publish images and film clips to my social media sites wherever I am in the world.

Chapter Thirteen

MAKING MOVIES

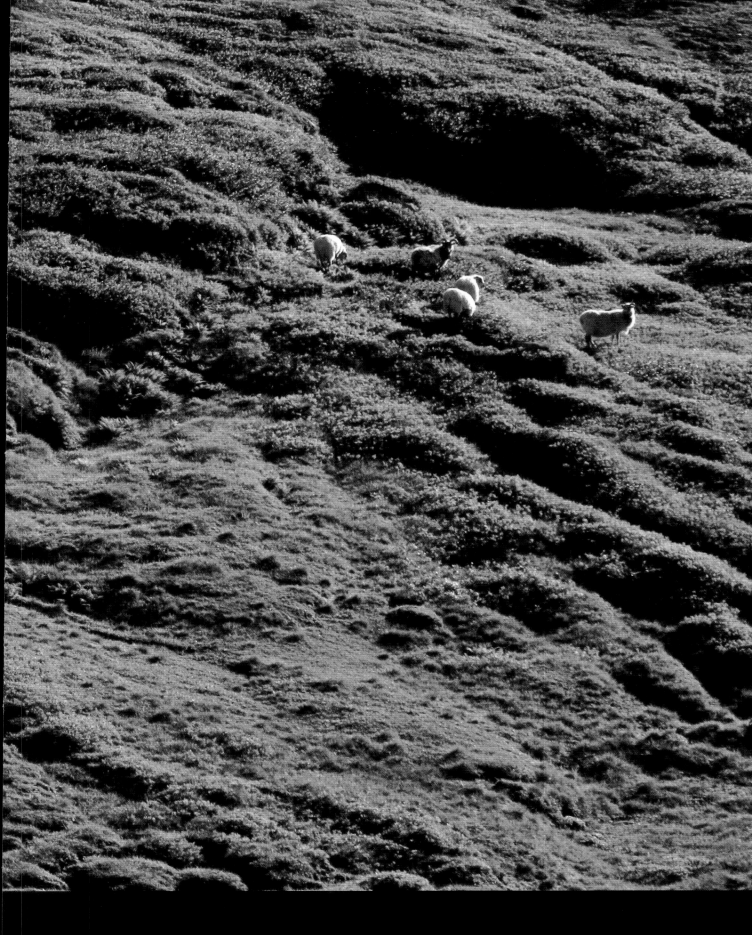

Perhaps the biggest change in DSLR cameras in the past few years has been the development of HD movie facilities. Canon was the first camera manufacturer to include a movie function in their cameras when they launched the 5D. According to DSLR guru, Philip Bloom, the movie function was included almost as an afterthought, a bonus feature thrown in simply 'because they could...' What Canon did not realise is that the feature would become a huge success. The quality of the movie files that can be recorded on the latest DSLR's is nothing short of staggering and is due to the incredible detail that the CMOS sensors in modern digital SLR's can capture.

The quality of the footage is very cinematic, due in the main to the use of stills camera lenses that deliver not only superb sharpness but also deliver a different 'feel' to the footage depending on the lens used and aperture selected. The footage is gorgeous because of the CMOS sensors but there are a few issues surrounding bit rates, compression and codecs that are being addressed as I write this. Since the technology is still being developed, DSLR's are nowhere near as user-friendly to film with as traditional camcorders. The footage that can be obtained with them, however, is unique, and for the stills photographer, the chance to use regular lenses to make movies without having to invest in new ones is a huge bonus.

The camera that started the DSLR revolution was the Canon 7D, quickly followed by the 5D mk2. These cameras produce beautiful footage and have been used to shoot some very high profile tv series such as 'House' and 'An Idiot Abroad.' Some of the scenes in the 'Iron Man 2' movie were also shot using them. This is a sobering thought when you consider that these are cameras within the budget of serious angling photographers.

BELOW
Jon Chappell filming in Mozambique. Thanks to DSLR technology, big rigs like this one are becoming things of the past.

Following hot on the heels of the C300 is a new pro DSLR from Canon, the 1DX. Whilst this camera features fewer megapixels than the 1DS Mk 3, it has a new sensor and the pixels are larger and better. The result is a camera that delivers amazing stills and sports incredible light gathering capabilities. The low light performance of these cameras is nothing short of staggering, allowing hand-held shots to be taken in almost darkness. An added bonus is a beefed-up movie function that can produce sumptuous footage and whilst it might not be quite as good for dedicated movie making as the C300 for those of us whom like to shoot both stills and HD movies, it is probably the ultimate all round camera.

The DSLR excels with lenses at the extreme ranges – wide angle and telephoto. With wide angle, the sense of 'space' is heightened and of course, the film maker can get close to subjects and yet still 'pull-in' the environment. I have filmed with both 14mm and 16-35mm lens and obtained beautiful, pin-sharp footage that has a unique look and feel. Similarly, with a long lens, the DSLR produces a stunning look thanks to the compressed depth of field that these lenses deliver. Don't forget, either, the potential for macro photography (albeit this is very tricky because of the focusing issues). And of course, you can use your lens filters, including polarisers, ND grads and your other favourites. Footage taken on a DSLR has a unique feel, due, in large part, to the use of lenses of different focal lengths and the potential to create different 'moods' by creative use of apertures.

DSLR's also excel in low light shooting. They produce footage that is way superior to film once the ISO speed goes above 1000. Some of the Nikon DSLR's can shoot noise-free footage at ISO25000 and the latest releases from Canon go to over ISO 100000!

The downside of shooting movies with DSLR camera bodies is that without some vital accessories, the camera is not easy to use. Since the image you are recording has to be seen through the camera's preview screen in 'live view mode,' getting exposures right on bright, sunny days is tricky and so too is focusing.

ABOVE
A modern DSLR camera pimped out with all the accessories to make it suitable for shooting movies. It has extra sound equipment in the form of a digital recorder, Rode mike, follow focus, Z-Finder view screen and Zacuto shoulder and pistol-grip frame.

Inevitably, the camera manufacturers have looked at the huge Indie film industry that is springing up around the 5D and decided that they will produce a movie camera with a DSLR sensor. The new Canon C300 is such a beast and there are two versions, one that is compatible with the Canon stills lenses and the other with their prime movie lenses. It is an amazing piece of kit that is going to become a huge hit since it addresses some of the niggling glitches with the DSLR film work such as sound inputs, bit rate, compression, frame rates and phenomenon such as 'rolling shutter.' Of course, it is not cheap at around 10000 pounds give or take but to put things into perspective, this is a camera that even serious movie makers will choose and it is a fraction of the cost of the serious movie cameras of yesteryear.

The number One accessory to make the camera much easier to focus is a viewfinder. These allow the camera to be used 'conventionally' whereby the operator looks into a viewfinder rather than a live-view screen. Companies such as Zacuto with their Z-finder products make the job easier.

Sound is also limited, at least on the camera's in-built microphone. Fortunately, there are plug-in sound accessories that fit into the camera's 'hot shoe' or input sockets that will remedy any issues with audio quality. To be honest, the built-in mic on the Canon DSLR's does a creditable job but if you want stereo sound, using hot-shoe mounted mikes and/or radio mikes is possible with a bolt mini sound unit that can be fitted to the base of the camera.

Perhaps the problem that DSLR's are most infamous for is 'rolling shutter,' a form of distortion that causes 'converging verticals (narrowing perspective)' when the camera is moved quickly. There are also some 'artefacting' issues in certain situations but they are relatively inconsequential unless you are producing footage for broadcast at the highest level. The latest C300 and 1DX have addressed these and other issues and the lower priced DSLR releases are bound to follow suit.

Pioneers like Philip Bloom have embraced filming with DSLR's and helped in the development of a host of accessories that resolve some of the issues revolving around focusing, smooth panning, pull focus and clarity of the 'live view' preview screen. I thoroughly recommend checking out Philip's website (it can be found on www.philipbloom.net) The site gives lots of sound advice about how to make movies and time lapse sequences as well as edit them. Philip also sells accessories for DSLR film makers, including a portable 'pocket dolly' system that makes it easy to create cinematic quality panning with the DSLR.

Zacuto are an interesting company that have produced a number of great accessories for DSLR movie making. These include harness and shoulder mounts that make the camera easy to hold steady when hand held and to pan with. These products are in a modular form featuring bolt on and off arms that allow you to pimp the camera out with all manner of useful

devices such as lighting, sound units, follow focus and monitors.

For smooth pull focus, a follow focus is a must. It is difficult to pull focus smoothly on a moving object but with a follow focus it is much easier. This is basically a gearing system and large handwheel that makes lens transitions vey smooth and much easier to execute.

There are a number of options regarding the resolution that your DSLR will record movies to. The highest resolution is full HD and produces footage of broadcast quality. The number of frames recorded per second will depend on the user settings but the standard output for most broadcast is around 24 or 25 depending on the country you live in. The output frame rate can be set at the editing stage. According to Philip Bloom, for regular daylight shooting the camera should be set up as follows.

Camera Settings for DSLR filming in daylight (modelled on 5D Mk2 Canon)

Set camera to manual

Set shutter speed of 1/50th of a second. This produces smooth footage that plays with a cinematic feel.

ISO to be set according to required aperture but the most noise-free ISO settings are based around ISO 160 and multiples thereof, ie: 160, 320, 640. Use an ND or polarising filter to hold back light if wide apertures are selected in good light.

User defined parameters to include contrast and sharpness to be dropped to lowest setting. This produces a rather flat looking image but one that is trouble free and can be tweaked in post production.

Although my experiments with DSLR movies are so far limited I can pass on a few tips when it comes to filming in angling scenarios. With a wide angle lens fitted, the camera can be tripod mounted but hand held allows you to move around. The camera's zoom will continue to work, so you can crash in and out as required.

Wide angle lenses produce peerless footage on 'blue sky' days when the lens is fitted with a polarising filter. By angling the

camera upward from a low filming position, the big blue sky dominates the image and the footage is very crisp indeed

With longer lenses it is possible to isolate subjects my using a shallow depth of field (set the camera to f2.8 or f4 with a shutter speed of 1/50th second. The ISO setting should be a multiple of 160). To achieve wide apertures at 1/50th of a second in strong light, it may be necessary to fit a polariser (where appropriate) or an ND filter to hold back enough light This produces beautiful, crisp images with defined edges. The focus can be shifted by turning the focus ring while the scene is being recorded, creating a 'pull focus' effect that brings foreground and background images in and out of focus. A classic example is framing up with some wild grasses in the foreground and an angle casting in the river in the distance – using a wide aperture and focusing on the grasses the focus is shifted to the angler, creating a beautiful and seamless shift that looks very professional.

Whether you use a DSLR, compact or camcorder to record fishing movies, the most essential discipline is to obtain enough sequences to 'tell a story.' A wide shot that simply runs from several minutes is very dull and boring. When you shoot the movies is very important to grab short sequences that help to link the story together and give you cutting points when the main footage loses focus, is badly framed or loses its way. These sections can help to explain where the action is taking place, at what time of year, what equipment is being used and so on. Taking the time to film these extra sections is the difference between recording an event (perhaps the capture of a fish) and telling a story.

A recent phenomenon in movie-making is the extension of still images to create time-lapse movies. It is a lot simpler than you might think to do this – simply mount the camera on a tripod, shoot stills over several minutes or hours and then convert them into a film using 'Quicktime.' These 'short' movies are fun and easy to make and have a unique feel. Once again, I can recommend Philip Bloom's website as a source of inspiration. Since as anglers we spend a great deal of time by the water, we have numerous opportunities to film time

Perhaps the camera with the biggest future in angling is the Go Pro Hero camera. This is an amazing little mini- camera that records stills, timelapse stills and HD movie footage. The cameras come with a choice of housings, one which allows sound and the other which allows the camera to be completely submerged in water. They are also supplied with a variety of mounts including head straps so that they can be worn like a head torch, chest harness, vehicle mount, tripod mount and mounts that can be affixed to mountain bikes and other sports equipment.

They are amazing cameras delivering a unique Anglers-eye viewpoint, making the viewer of the footage they produce feel that they are present during the shoot. Because they are so compCt, versatile and robust they can be worn and used almost anywhere. Strap two of the new Hero2's side by side and facing forward and back and you get 360 degree footage! The feel of Go Pro footage is quite unique and gritty - it is perfect for capturing raw fishing footage that has drama and excitement. For online tutorials about fishing tackle and for capturing blog-style footage for social media and websites, these cameras are the perfect tool. I love them! I will also make a brave prediction that within five years Go Pro cameras will become a standard piece of Kit for serious anglers everywhere...

Should this book become successful enough to go into re-print, I can envisage that the section that will require the most updating will be this one. Most likely, the second edition of Fisheye will be a digital book with movie tutorials and film clips. The power of movie-making on DSLR has handed film making over to millions of people like myself whom would not normally have the money or the equipment to make high quality HD films. At the time of writing, we stand on the threshold of a new era in photography when, using the same equipment, we can produce still images, time-lapse movies and full HD movies to a standard that even five years ago we could only dream about. The future for photography and film-making is a very exciting one indeed and as anglers we have been empowered to record and share the fishing experience and share it with the world. Good luck!

ABOVE

This is the viewpoint created by the Go Pro camera. It's a unique angler's eye viewpoint and is created by wearing the camera either on a special harness, either strapped to the head like a head torch or to the chest. The result is intimate, raw and exciting video suitable for blog

lapse sequences of sunrises, sunsets, boatyards and weather events to name but a few topics.

To make time-lapse movies, you will need to download Quicktime and use the option from the file menu 'open image sequence.' To shoot the stills, you will need to use a device known as an 'intervalometer.' These take the form of remote cords that plug into the camera that can be programmed to shoot stills at defined intervals. The operator dials in the number of exposures and the time between each exposure. With the camera set either to manual (or if the light changes, AV mode is probably best), the intervalometer can be set to take literally hundreds of J-Peg stills. It is also possible to shoot raw files, batch process them in post-production and export them as J-Pegs into a folder using Lightroom

ACKNOWLEDGEMENTS

My Dad - he taught me everything I know (so he tells everyone!)

My grandfathers, Lou Hayes and Dave Massey along with my Uncle Colin Ellingham for putting up with me on all those fishing trips of my youth and helping me to become a fisherman. The world is a lonelier place without you all.

My Nan Massey - for buying me my first fishing rod. I miss you so much...

Stewart Allum for shaping my fishing career.

To my friends whom have stood in uncomfortable positions for ridiculous periods of time, especially Ed 'Scoops' Brown whose patience is verging on saintly.

Gareth Owen for helping me out and contributing to some truly memorable shoots.

Mick Brown for being such a great photographic subject and partner and co-star of so many rip-roaring adventures.

Peter Stone and Bob Church for teaching me that great anglers should have humility.

Clive Gammon for proving that great angling prose don't need to be flowery.

Jon Chappell for all those great film shoots and helpful advice.

Mick Rouse and Lloyd Rogers at Bauer for sharing their expertise and encouraging me.

Simeon Bond for giving me my first-break as a pro angler when he was at Shimano.

And to Richard Lee for giving me the platform to exhibit my work in Angling Times on a regular basis.

And finally, to everyone whom puts up with me, especially my wife Anne Marit and my wonderful children Danny, Jessica, Josh and Alice...